MEDICARE SIMPLIFIED

EXPERT ADVICE WITH REAL EXAMPLES TO UNDERSTAND YOUR OPTIONS, AVOID PITFALLS, AND CONFIDENTLY CHOOSE THE RIGHT PLAN

ANNE N. KNOWLER

CONTENTS

INTRODUCTION

Each month, I engage with hundreds of seniors and their family members navigating the complexities of Medicare enrollment. Many express feelings of anxiety, stress, confusion, and even dread. If you're feeling this way, know that it's completely normal. It's understandable to question why such an important process can be so perplexing. A significant reason is that health insurance, social security, and Medicare education are not provided in our typical learning environments -- not in high schools, the military, or colleges. Our healthcare providers and their staff don't have the time to explain these concepts, and often, they have the same questions due to the fast rate of change in the industry. Too many of the Medicare conversations I had in 2024 included someone saying, "I'm so confused and don't know what to do." This confusion often robs people of sleep and peace of mind, even though Medicare is meant to provide comfort and security.

I enjoy speaking with my clients, listening to their stories, and understanding their needs. I feel like I'm serving others when I explain how different plans can protect them financially. The best part is their genuine appreciation and gratitude for my help. This book provides a simplified version of Medicare based upon hundreds of conversations I have every year with real people across 28 states. I want to reduce your stress and give you a fresh perspective about Medicare. As a licensed health insurance agent, I aim to share my hands-on experience and practical approach. Hopefully, you'll find this information in a clear, accessible manner, free from technical jargon, acronyms, and confusing dumps of information.

This guide is designed for older adults, especially those new to Medicare, who want to start from the beginning. It's also a valuable resource for family members and caregivers assisting seniors with Medicare decisions. Together, we will cover the basics of how and when to enroll, explore different options like Original Medicare and Medicare Advantage, and address common misunderstandings that often arise during the Medicare journey. I aim to help you feel knowledgeable, confident, and prepared to make informed Medicare decisions. I promise this will be easy to understand.

I must address the topic of technology upfront. Approximately 8.8% of U.S. households—around 11.5 million homes—lack a home internet connection (Finley Engineering Company, n.d.). Although this shows significant progress, based only on my experience, I estimate that most of those households consist of senior citizens. If you are a senior with zero or low technology in the home, have no fear; you can find plenty of assistance over the phone or in person. If you would like my help, find someone to email me at **Anne@AdviserAnne.com**. Ask them to write that you are requesting a phone call from me. If I am not licensed in your state, I will connect you with someone I trust.

This book will have repetition, which will help reinforce key concepts. I once heard in a training environment that we need to hear something 48 times before remembering it. That's not happening here, but you'll hear repetition as we delve into more detail throughout the book. I'm intentionally avoiding excessive specifics because there are thousands of unique scenarios based on a person's location, financial situation, health concerns, and providers. This book is more of an overview for beginners or a refresher for those considering a change in their coverage. It's not intended to be a manual or textbook but a realistic conversation to answer questions I hear all day long when assisting my clients. The goal is to empower you with knowledge and confidence, whether you enroll yourself online or work with a licensed agent.

1

THE EASY BASICS

Let's start with the topic of mindset. The other day, I spoke with a gentleman named Frank. Frank is a retired industrial engineer who worked at three companies during his long career. He confessed to me, with both embarrassment and frustration, that he found Medicare utterly bewildering. "How," he asked, "can something so crucial to my health and well-being be so difficult to understand?"

My conversation with Frank is not unique. It's what I hear from callers every day. After years of contributing to society, working hard, and planning for retirement, he finds himself at a loss when navigating Medicare. This lack of clarity often leads to unnecessary anxiety, yet it's perfectly normal to feel stressed; after all, Medicare isn't something discussed socially or within families because, deep down, everyone knows they don't know much about it. Or, you may be thinking, *I'm already in a plan that's working well for me, so why do I need to learn more?* or perhaps, *Isn't Medicare a set-it-and-*

forget-it insurance situation? These are common questions that make sense. Once you've turned 65 and enrolled in Medicare Part A, Part B, and a Part D plan, it seems like the logical conclusion would be that you're all set. I genuinely wish it were that simple. However, the reality is a bit more complex. You will periodically be dealing with changes.

My key takeaway about mindset is that you are not marrying these plans. Nothing is set in stone. For example, if you are a Medicare Advantage person you can make a change every year during the Annual Enrollment Period. I don't recommend it, but you understand my point. Please take a break from the unnecessary stress and anxiety. If you try a plan for a year and it doesn't work out, then you'll make a change during the next relevant enrollment period. The exception to this thinking is that some folks on Original Medicare with Supplement plans worry about changing plans because they might not be able to re-enroll in their old Supplement if they change their mind. I'll dive into this more in a bit.

For many, the fear surrounding Medicare is rooted in past experiences with health insurance when options were less accessible, and preexisting conditions could lead to denial of coverage. Enrolling in Medicare might dredge up memories of financial hardship or difficult choices made in the name of health coverage. However, let's acknowledge that times have changed. New laws and protections mean that the healthcare landscape is vastly different now. You have rights and options that didn't exist before. Embrace this moment as an opportunity to shed those old fears. As you explore the options available, approach it with a mindset open to learning. You may find that choosing a plan becomes less of a chore and more of an empowering experience.

The other mindset problem I hear constantly is the ever-present American paranoia that somehow you are going to get screwed over. My heartfelt advice to you regarding Medicare, from one skeptic to another, is that you should lose all preconceived notions that someone is trying to rob or rip you off. If you have paranoia or profound fears of the medical insurance industry setting out to ruin you financially or kill you medically, please take a break from that thinking for a minute. Please consider the possibility that this is a tremendous benefit you've earned by working for decades. Once on Medicare, you are covered one way or another by doctors and hospitals that accept Medicare. This is the most widely used, legally scrutinized, lawfully guarded, and contractually bound government program in the United States. More than 65 million people in the United States are enrolled in Medicare (U.S. Centers for Medicare and Medicaid Services, n.d.). This includes individuals aged 65 and older, as well as younger individuals with disabilities or specific conditions such as End-Stage Renal Disease (ESRD) and Amyotrophic Lateral Sclerosis (ALS).

That said, I hope you'll finish this book, so you have a good high-level overview that allows you to feel more comfortable when changes happen. Allow me to explain.

1.1 CHANGE IS CONSTANT

The only thing you can count on in the world of Medicare is that everything will change sooner or later. Insurance companies update their plans and sometimes even discontinue plans altogether. Also, changes occur with doctors, hospitals, medical groups, and other providers. For instance, your insurance carrier's contract with a medical group you love may end; therefore, you must find a new plan to remain with your doctor. Speaking of doctors and specialists, they move around too—sometimes to a different medical group and sometimes to a different state or across the country. Sometimes, they retire. Clients often know the doctor or practice they'd like to move to when this happens, but they need a different Medicare plan. Sometimes, you may want or need to move as well. You'll need to enroll in a plan accepted at your new location whenever you change your permanent residence. I'll address more potential changes and their specifics in later chapters. Still, I want to let you know that most of my clients connect with me because something has changed, and they need a new plan.

1.2 SIMPLIFIED OVERVIEW

Since 1965, Medicare has been a stalwart federal health insurance program for people aged 65 and over and younger individuals with disabilities. Medicare described in its simplest form consists of four main components. Part A is hospital insurance, Part B is medical insurance, Part C plans are Medicare Advantage, and Part D is prescription drug coverage. By law, at age 65, we all go on Medicare Parts A (hospital) and B (medical). Some people can delay enrollment in Parts A and B if they have credible coverage from elsewhere, such as an employer; I'll explain later. However, most folks are happy to go on Parts A and B at the same time around their 65th birthday. They must also enroll in drug coverage as soon as they are eligible.

Medicare Part A primarily covers **hospital insurance**, including inpatient hospital stays, skilled nursing facility care, hospice care, and limited home health care services. It helps cover room, board, and necessary medical services during hospital stays but does not cover long-term or custodial care.

Medicare Part B covers medically **necessary care and services**, such as outpatient care or doctor visits. For example, when you see your primary care doctor for your annual physical, vaccinations, screenings or unexpected illness... those are Part B visits. Generally, you will have zero copay for most preventive services if they are received from a doctor or other qualified health care professional.

As I go through a few more summary details, in this section of the book I'm only speaking about most people eligible for Medicare, not those on Medicaid nor Americans in the highest tax brackets. Also, a key term to explain is **beneficiary**. When discussing Medicare, a beneficiary is an individual who is eligible for and enrolled in Medicare, receiving healthcare coverage under Medicare Part A, Part B or Part C (Medicare Advantage), or Part D (prescription drug coverage). Beneficiaries include seniors aged 65 and older, as well as certain younger individuals with disabilities or specific medical conditions. The beneficiary is ***you*** (the patient, so to speak) or the senior you are assisting.

Again, at age 65, individuals are eligible for Medicare if they are U.S. citizens or lawful permanent residents who have lived in the U.S. for at least five continuous years. Additionally, they must meet work history requirements (typically 40 work credits) or qualify through a current or former spouse's work history to receive premium-free Part A. Those without sufficient work credits can still enroll but may have to pay a premium for Part A coverage. For beneficiaries with limited income and resources, depending on where you live, there may be state resources available to help pay Medicare monthly premiums. More on that later.

Most Medicare recipients have 40-quarters of work credits from their work or their spouse's work. Again, Medicare Part A is for hospital coverage, for which most people will pay $0 monthly. However, we all pay a standard monthly premium for Medicare Part B, which is medical coverage. In 2025, as I am writing this, the monthly premium for Part B is $185.00. Most people aren't aware of this expense because it's coming out of their Social Security Retirement benefit every month; it's coming out of that check before the funds are deposited into their account.

We enroll in Medicare Parts A and B through the Social Security Administration after creating a Social Security account at **www.ssa.gov**. Forevermore, think of your Medicare and Social Security profiles being permanently entwined because they are. Once you've created your Social Security account and logged in, you can check your eligibility for Medicare Parts A and B. Creating this online account is now required and gives you easy access to manage your Medicare and Social Security benefits anytime. If you need help, call Social Security at **1-800-772-1213** or visit the local office. I'll be discussing exceptions in later chapters but one of the biggest exceptions to the "basics" is that permanently disabled folks are automatically enrolled in Medicare Parts A and B after being on disability payments for two years. This is rarely explained to them.

Therefore, they often don't know how they ended up on Medicare, and sometimes they don't know their options going forward.

Most people on Permanent Social Security Disability Insurance (SSDI) are required to pay the Medicare Part B premium, just like retirees on Medicare. Again, when approved for SSDI, you're generally eligible for Medicare after a 24-month waiting period. Once enrolled in Medicare Part B, the premium is usually deducted directly from your monthly SSDI benefits. The exceptions are low-income individuals with limited resources; they may qualify for a Medicare Savings Program (MSP), which can help pay the Part B premium. Some states cover Medicare premiums for individuals with disabilities who meet certain income and resource limits. If unsure, contact your local Social Security office or your state Medicaid program to determine your Part B premium assistance eligibility.

An important piece of the puzzle to mention here is how geographic location, where you live, will decide most of your Medicare options, especially when considering Medicare Advantage plans. All health insurance availability depends on your zip code and county and Medicare works the same way. Where you live is called your Service Area. Insurance companies offer various plans in different service areas, and the specifics can vary dramatically. When enrolling, you'll need to provide your residential zip code and county, as this determines what plans are available to you. Your permanent residence address will be required. A PO Box address can only be used for receiving your Medicare related mail. No matter how rural, a home address will be required for enrollment and plan selections.

So, summarizing in the smallest nutshell as it pertains to ***most folks.*** By law, we all go on Medicare Part A (Hospital) and Part B (Medical) when we turn 65 years old, and for the rest of our lives, we pay a Part B monthly premium out of our Social Security check. Those are the starting facts. To put this in perspective, many middle-aged folks look forward to going on Medicare; they can't wait! Despite being on employer plans for decades, it's the most secure health insurance they'll ever experience.

1.2.1 CMS (Centers for Medicare & Medicaid Services)

CMS (Centers for Medicare & Medicaid Services) is a federal agency within the U.S. Department of Health and Human Services (HHS) that is responsible for administering key national healthcare programs, including Medicare, Medicaid, the Children's Health Insurance Program (CHIP), and the Health Insurance Marketplace.

CMS is responsible for policy development and oversight of the programs to ensure compliance. They also manage and process payments and reimbursements to healthcare providers and organizations. CMS collects and analyzes healthcare data to monitor trends, improve quality, and inform policy decisions.

Lastly, they are our consumer protection for Medicare—safeguarding our rights as beneficiaries, promoting transparency, and addressing fraud, waste, and abuse in healthcare. CMS plays a central role in shaping the U.S. healthcare system by regulating healthcare access, costs, and quality for millions of Americans. For comprehensive information about CMS programs and services, visit CMS.gov.

1.3 PAYING FOR MEDICARE PART B

1.3.1 Automatic Payments

Paying your Medicare Part B premiums directly from your Social Security retirement income is not required, but it's the most common and convenient option to ensure your Part B coverage is not accidentally terminated for lack of payment. I've assisted a few people who thought they would treat this monthly expense like a bill they could resist, delay, or ignore. They regretted it and wished someone had explained how serious the Medicare system is. They experienced a great deal of financial and medical hassle. Eventually, they got back on track with the help of their local Social Security office.

If you started receiving Social Security retirement benefits before age 65, you will be automatically enrolled in Medicare Parts A and B when you become eligible for Medicare at age 65.

If you are not receiving Social Security retirement before age 65 (you delayed your retirement benefits), you will manually enroll in Medicare through your SSA.gov account, as previously explained.

In both scenarios, after your successful enrollment in Parts A and B you will still have choices to make, most importantly how you'll receive your prescription drug coverage.

1.3.2 Direct Payments

Nowadays, many retirees delay receiving their Social Security retirement income until well after age 65. In that case, they must pay their Medicare Part B premium directly. Here's the important reminder: If you miss Part B monthly premium payments, your Medicare coverage could be terminated.

Here are the options:

1. **Direct Billing (Medicare Premium Bill)**:
    a. Medicare will send you a "Medicare Premium Bill" (CMS-500).
    b. The bill is typically sent quarterly (every three months), but you can request monthly billing.
2. **Payment Methods for the Medicare Premium Bill**:
    a. **Online Payment**: You can pay your premium through your Medicare account at Medicare.gov.
    b. **Bank Account Withdrawal**: Schedule payments using your bank's online bill pay service.
3. **Check or Money Order**: Send a check or money order to the address on your bill.
4. **Medicare Easy Pay**: Sign up for automatic payments, deducting the premium directly from your monthly bank account. This method is strongly recommended to ensure payments are made on time, and to prevent coverage gaps.
5. **Automatic Deduction from a Railroad Retirement Board (RRB) Check**: If you receive benefits from the RRB instead of Social Security, your premiums can be deducted directly from those payments.

If you need assistance setting up payments, Medicare customer service or the Social Security Administration can help.

To conclude the discussion of the Part B monthly premium, I want to emphasize that no matter which approach you take going forward, whether Original Medicare or Medicare Advantage, you will always pay the Part B monthly premium.

1.4 THE TWO APPROACHES TO MEDICARE

There are two different approaches for you to consider after you've enrolled in Medicare Part A and B: Medicare Advantage vs. Original Medicare. It's fascinating how polarized people can sound on this topic without citing any specifics. I will meet people who tell me, "I would never, ever use a Medicare Advantage Plan." When I ask why, they usually have zero idea why, or they'll say, "Because *my favorite newspaper* wrote an article stating the Advantage approach is bad." I spoke with an Original Medicare person just last week who could not afford a Supplement plan, so she's been trying to survive with only Medicare Part A and Part B and a Part D plan for drugs. Of course, without a Supplement plan, she's been struggling with medical bills. The ONLY reason she never tried an Advantage plan was because someone told her she would lose all freedom to see her choice of doctors and specialists. That's categorically false information in her scenario. At least three different Medicare Advantage insurance carriers offer Advantage PPO plans in her service area that her doctors accepted. So, I highly recommend that you remain completely open-minded regarding which approach is best for you until all options in your service area have been explored.

1.4.1 Original Medicare

When a person has enrolled in Medicare Parts A and B and a standalone prescription drug plan officially called Part D, this approach is referred to as "Original Medicare." Folks on Original Medicare must enroll in a standalone Part D plan for prescription coverage and they usually get a Medigap policy as well. Like everyone else, Original Medicare beneficiaries must enroll in a Part D plan as soon as they become eligible to avoid late penalties later one. It's easy to remember Part D because D is for drugs, but it's a daily occurrence that someone tells me they didn't know they were supposed to enroll in a Part D plan. It's also important that Original Medicare beneficiaries know the importance of enrolling in a Medigap plan as soon as possible for financial reasons. These policies are also referred to as Supplement plans. Again, the Medigap and Supplement plans refer to the same thing which is extra coverage Original Medicare people enroll in to cover out-of-pocket costs not paid for by Medicare A or B. Original Medicare covers many hospital and medical services but sometimes does not pay entirely for everything. Supplement plans are offered by private insurance companies to fill in the gaps left by the standard Parts A and B coverage. As of 2025, there are 9 Medicare Supplement (Medigap) plans available for new enrollees in the United States. Supplement plans are typically available for enrollment year-round however some plans require medical underwriting. In Chapter 6 the plans are listed with summary details.

Summarizing this section: If you stay on Original Medicare, you will also need to enroll in a standalone prescription drug plan called Part D. Technically, you could stop there, but it's not recommended. Medicare Supplement plans are available to beneficiaries who are enrolled in Original Medicare. These medigap policies are secondary insurance coverage to original Medicare and will help you pay for deductibles, co-insurance and copays, and may cover services that aren't covered by Original Medicare.

1.4.2 Medicare Advantage

The other approach is Medicare Advantage, also known as Medicare Part C. A Medicare Advantage plan is an all-in-one alternative to Original Medicare. It covers everything that Medicare Part A (hospital insurance) and Part B (medical insurance) cover, plus prescription drug coverage (Part D). You'll see these plans referred to as MAPD plans. There are some Medicare Advantage plans (MA only) without drug coverage included. These are great for veterans who get their meds from the VA, for example. Many Medicare Advantage plans offer additional benefits, such as dental, vision, hearing, and various incentive programs. Private insurance companies approved by Medicare provide these plans within familiar structures, such as HMOs and PPOs. We'll go into deeper detail on Advantage plans in later chapters.

As we discussed earlier, by law, you are now registered for Medicare Parts A and B online in your **https://www.ssa.gov/** account or at the local Social Security office, or you were automatically enrolled in them. That's the starting point. You now have Medicare Parts A and B, and that's your ticket to choosing the Original Medicare approach or picking out a Medicare Advantage plan. No matter which direction you go in, you will always have Parts A and B, even if you feel they are only lurking in the background. For example, some Medicare Advantage (Part C) people think they are no longer tied to Parts A and B, but that's not entirely accurate. You are ***only eligible*** for a Medicare Advantage Plan if you are already enrolled in Parts A and B. Parts A and B are the foundation of your Medicare coverage and will be with you for life.

So far, we've covered how once enrolled in Medicare Parts A and B, you can choose between two different approaches: Stay on Original Medicare or become a Medicare Advantage member. There is no wrong answer here; both approaches work for millions of Americans. It depends on where you live, your medical concerns, and what plans your doctor or medical group accepts.

As we wrap up this introductory overview, I hope you now feel more comfortable knowing there are two approaches to Medicare, and that you're comfortable moving deeper into detail. Why continue reading? Here's the thing: Life changes, and so do your medical needs. The plan that suits you today may not be the best choice tomorrow. Your health has changed, or your financial situation is different from when you first enrolled. You need new treatments or medications that your current plan doesn't cover. Understanding the full range of Medicare options allows you to adapt to these changes efficiently and effectively, ensuring you're always covered in the way that best suits your needs.

You will often read that it is "critical, crucial, imperative that you research every detail to create a tailored plan just for you." That messaging confuses people. You do not need to become an expert, and no plans are designed specifically for you. All medical insurance plans are set in stone by the time we see them; they are not ala carte menus from which we can select features. Clients will sometimes say "can't you remove that benefit because I will never use it?" That is not how health insurance works and Medicare is health insurance. You only need to understand enough to let an expert help you, or so you feel comfortable enrolling online. Plans with specific features will be available in your service area. You can speak with a licensed agent to choose an approach, explore different plans, and complete your enrollments. All options will largely be based on your location.

In conclusion, understanding Medicare is not just about checking a box and moving on. It is also about engaging with a system that can be as dynamic as life. By educating yourself about the ins and outs of Medicare, you will equip yourself with the knowledge to navigate its complexities confidently. This knowledge is empowering, transforming what might initially seem daunting into an opportunity to take control of your health and future. So, as you move forward in this book, remember that the effort you invest in understanding Medicare is an investment in your well-being and peace of mind.

1.5 TIMING IS EVERYTHING

As we all know, timing is crucial in many aspects of life, and enrolling in Medicare is no exception. The Initial Enrollment Period (IEP) is when you first become eligible for Medicare. It's a seven-month window that surrounds your 65th birthday. Specifically, it includes the three months before and three months after the month you turn 65, as well as the month of your birthday. This period is your opportunity to enroll in Medicare, ensuring your healthcare coverage begins as smoothly as possible. Missing this window can lead to challenges, so understanding its significance is key to avoiding unnecessary complications.

To enroll during the IEP, you'll need to take a few deliberate steps. Start by reaching out to Social Security, as they handle Medicare Parts A and B registration. You can register online at **https://www.ssa.gov/** or over the phone, or in person at your local Social Security office. It's a straightforward process, but having all your personal information ready, such as your Social Security number is essential. Remember, enrolling during this period secures your health coverage and helps you avoid potential late penalties, which can unnecessarily increase your costs. This proactive step ensures you're covered without gaps and offers peace of mind, knowing you have healthcare insurance.

As you journey through Medicare, remember that resources for ongoing support are always within reach. Medicare.gov (**https://www.medicare.gov/**) is a helpful website for researching your Medicare options.. I highly recommend you create an account there in addition to your SSA.gov account. It's critical that you use the exact same name, spelling and precision that you use when creating your SSA.gov account. Local Medicare counseling services can offer personalized advice tailored to your unique situation and location. Also, licensed health insurance agents are a good resource for advice as you approach 65 years old. It's always better to ask questions in advance rather than too late. These services provide a human touch, offering informed and empathetic guidance.

1.5.1 Late Penalties

I provide this section now to reinforce the importance of asking questions and examining your options early. Penalties are real but this topic should not cause you sleepless nights. I take the case that having read or listened to this book, you will readily know when to enroll in Medicare Parts A, B and D. Also, thanks to modern online resources such as SSA.gov and Medicare.gov, most people today do not struggle with getting their Medicare enrollment done on time. If you do not stick your head in the sand and ignore all mail and notices, you will easily avoid late penalties. However, I must provide this information as reminder that planning and acting around your Medicare enrollment opportunities is vital for financial sensibility – no one wants to pay 10% extra for something when it was completely avoidable. Please help me spread the word.

Again, a person approaching their 65th birthday must have a Social Security account, or they can go to their local Social Security Administration office to register for Medicare Parts A and B. If you have access to the internet, I highly recommend you go to SSA.gov and then click on "Apply for

Benefits." Usually, this is when most 65 year olds enroll in Part A and B, at the same time. If you or your spouse are still working, you may be able to wait to sign up for Medicare without paying a late enrollment penalty. However, if you are still working you must check with your Employer's plan administrator because sometimes they will require you to enroll in Part A and B as soon as you are eligible. It all depends on your Employer's plan's requirements. If you are self-employed or have health insurance that's not available to everyone at the company (such as retiree coverage), ask your insurance carrier if your coverage is an employer group health plan. If it's not you'll need to sign up for Medicare Parts A and B when you turn 65. These are just some of the examples of why it's so important that you know the rules of your employer or retirement coverage. The employer may offer coverage when you have Medicare such as drug plans, supplemental plans or even Medicare Advantage plans. Sometimes retirement plans offer a monthly allowance or stipend toward your Medicare options, but you still need to select a plan from carriers operating in your service area. ***Always check.***

If for some unforeseen reason you do not enroll when you become eligible here are the penalties you may incur.

Part A

The Part A late penalty is 10% of your monthly premium for twice the number of years that you could have been enrolled but weren't. For example, let's say you missed enrolling in Part A for 4 years. 4 times 2 equals 8 years. If your Part A premium is $300/month, the penalty would be 10% of that which is $30 per month. You'll pay $330 per month for the next 8 years.

Part B

The Medicare Part B late enrollment penalty is 10% for each full 12-month period you could have had Part B but didn't sign up. This penalty is added to your monthly premium for as long as you have Part B. In this scenario you were 2 full years late signing up and the standard Part B monthly premium is $185 per month. 10% per year times 2 years equals 20%. 20% of $185 equals $37 per month. $185 plus $37 means you are paying $222 per month for as long as you have Medicare Part B.

Part D

The Medicare Part D late enrollment penalty is 1% of the national base beneficiary premium for each full month you went without creditable prescription drug coverage after being eligible. This penalty is added to your monthly Part D premium permanently. This applies when first enrolling in Part D, or when you have spent at least 63 days without drug coverage.

This is a common scenario so I'm listing the calculation steps as clearly as possible. Right now, the National Base Beneficiary Premium is $36.78 per month. Let's say you are 15 months late enrolling in Part D prescription coverage.

- The penalty percentage is 1% per month × 15 months = 15%
- The penalty amount is 15% of $36.78 = $5.52

- The penalty amount of $5.52 rounded to the nearest $0.10 is $5.50 per month.
- Total Monthly Premium will be your plan's premium + $5.50

So, if your monthly Part D premium is $41 per month, instead you'll be paying $46.50 every month. No matter which drug plan you select, even if it's under $20 per month, you'll always be paying the extra $5.50 every month.

This chapter explored a large array of basics that could contribute to you transforming your Medicare experience from daunting to manageable. As we learned, acknowledging the emotional aspects, equipping yourself with the right tools, and seeking continuous support are all steps that can empower you in this journey. Next, we will delve into additional foundational aspects of Medicare, providing you with the building blocks necessary to navigate this essential system with confidence and clarity.

2

MEDICARE ELIGIBILITY AND ENROLLMENT

We've discussed how Medicare is one of those inevitable parts of life. Throughout your Medicare journey, you'll encounter a myriad of details—some may seem arbitrary or frustratingly rigged against you. It's essential to recognize that these rules exist not to confuse you, but to ensure consistency and fairness across the board. Many clients ask me questions that seem to probe at the essence of Medicare: "Why are things this way?" they ask. The truth is some questions have no satisfying answer but please remember this: Medicare isn't health insurance you can game or outsmart by trying to buck the system. It's designed with specific rules and protections that provide workability for all eligible beneficiaries.

When you enroll in Medicare, honesty is your best policy. You might wonder if there's a way to secure a better deal by emphasizing your good health or lack of medication needs. Unfortunately, Medicare doesn't operate on individual exceptions. It's a standardized system where everyone follows the same rules. This might seem impersonal, but it's designed to be equitable. If you fear the system might fail you, take a step back. Consider the immense benefit you're accessing, earned through years of hard work and contributions. Medicare is a cornerstone of American healthcare, intricately woven into the lives of over 65 million people, including seniors and those with disabilities. It's a system built on decades of legal scrutiny and contractual obligations, offering nationwide coverage from doctors and hospitals. Enrolling during the proper enrollment periods is the best example of the Medicare rules.

2.1 UNDERSTANDING ELIGIBILITY

At its core, Medicare serves as a beacon of hope for those entering a new phase of life or facing specific health challenges. To make sense of your eligibility, begin with age requirements. If you're nearing 65, then you are about to qualify for Medicare. This milestone brings the opportunity to enroll in Medicare. Yet, age is not the only criterion. If you're under 65, but have a qualifying disability, or a condition like End-Stage Renal Disease or Amyotrophic Lateral Sclerosis (ALS), then you can also be eligible. These conditions fast-track eligibility, recognizing the immediate need for healthcare support. It's about ensuring that those in need have a safety net. Understanding these criteria can ease your path into Medicare, knowing it's designed to be inclusive and supportive.

As we've discussed, employment history also plays a critical role in your Medicare eligibility. It's not just about your current health status or age; it's about the work credits you've accumulated over your career. Medicare Part A covers hospital insurance and is often premium-free if you or your current or former spouse have sufficient work history—40 credits to be precise, which typically equates to about 10 years of work. If you haven't accrued enough credits, then you may purchase Part A, but a premium will apply. This is where knowing your work history becomes crucial. Imagine a scenario where someone took extended time off work or had inconsistent employment—this could impact their eligibility for premium-free Part A. Understanding your work history ensures that you can plan accordingly and avoid surprises.

The easiest way to look at your eligibility is to create an account at **www.ssa.gov.** Once you log into your account one of the first items you will see on the first page is the **Eligibility and Earnings** section. You can't miss it. It's listed before the Retirement Calculator.

If you are not comfortable with technology, you can have a trustworthy adult relative or helper do this with you if they have a laptop or desktop computer. Whenever possible it's best to create these accounts online. However, this should be done with meticulous attention to detail, and you must use the exact name on your Social Security card. When creating your ssa.gov account it will require you to verify your identity. Again, if you do not have technology, you can visit the local Social Security office and receive in-person assistance. If you are still working or using retirement medical coverage, it's critical that you know the Medicare rules for those plans before doing anything. Clients sometimes ask, "should I just sign up for Part A at 65 years old even if I am still working?" It all depends on the employer or retirement coverage you plan to remain in. If you have retiree coverage from a previous job, it may not pay for your health services if you don't have both Medicare Parts A and B.

Ask your benefits administrator how your retiree coverage works with Medicare. If no one in the HR department has a definite answer call the insurance company itself and ask an expert. It's important. Once you stop working at a company that provided credible health coverage you have an 8-month Special Enrollment Period (SEP) when you can sign up for Medicare (or add Part B to existing Part A coverage).

2.2 DUAL ELIGIBILITY

We cover this topic in Chapter 5 but for now I'd like to introduce the term Dual Eligibility. **Medicare Dual Eligibility** refers to individuals who qualify for both Medicare and Medicaid benefits. These individuals, known as "dual-eligible beneficiaries," typically have low income and limited resources. People often confuse the two different programs because the words are so similar. **Medicaid** is the state and federally funded program that provides health coverage to eligible low-income individuals and families. Medicaid is designed to help low-income families, children, pregnant women, elderly individuals, and people with disabilities. Benefits vary by state but typically include hospital services, doctor visits, nursing home care, and some prescription drugs. A helpful way to remember the difference is knowing that approximately 73 million people are on Medicaid but ***not*** Medicare, including low-income children, pregnant women, working-age adults, and individuals with disabilities who have not yet qualified for Medicare.

This is another layer of opportunity within Medicare. This dual status can ease financial strain, particularly for those with limited income and resources. Consider contacting your state's Medicaid office to determine if you are dual-eligible. They can provide personalized guidance based on your financial situation and health needs. Dual eligibility can be a vital lifeline for some seniors.

For those who qualify for both Medicare and Medicaid, dual eligibles, the insurance companies offer Special Needs Plans (SNPs) specifically designed to support these individuals.

2.2.1 Special Needs Plans

Special Needs Plans (SNPs) are a type of Medicare Advantage (Part C) plan designed specifically for individuals with unique healthcare needs. These plans provide tailored benefits, provider networks, and drug formularies to better serve their members. We've already mentioned the Special Needs Plan for Dual Eligibles but there are others. There are three main types of SNPs. Here's a brief description of each.

Dual Eligible SNPs (D-SNPs): For individuals who qualify for both Medicare and Medicaid (dual-eligible beneficiaries). These plans coordinate benefits to reduce out-of-pocket costs.

Chronic Condition SNPs (C-SNPs): For those with specific severe or disabling chronic conditions like diabetes, heart disease, or chronic lung disorders.

Institutional SNPs (I-SNPs): For individuals who live in nursing homes or require an equivalent level of care.

SNPs offer coordinated care, specialized provider networks, and tailored benefits to improve health outcomes for their members.

2.3 ENROLLMENT PERIODS

We've analyzed the importance of Medicare enrollment deadlines and how missing them can lead to financial penalties and can leave you vulnerable to gaps in your healthcare coverage. Imagine needing medical attention and discovering that your insurance won't start for several months. It's a scenario best avoided by adhering to these key enrollment periods. Late enrollment penalties can add up quickly, particularly for Part B, which can increase significantly the longer you delay. These penalties are permanent and will affect your budget in the long term, so it's worth taking the necessary steps to avoid them. Gaps in coverage can also result in unexpected medical expenses, which can be financially and emotionally stressful. Mark dates on a calendar, put a bookmark in this section, or tear the page out and put it on your refrigerator—whatever it takes for you to remember these enrollment periods.

For those of you who use technology, setting calendar reminders on your phone or computer can be a simple yet effective way to ensure you don't miss relevant dates. Medicare offers online tools that alert you to upcoming deadlines based on your personal enrollment timeline. These reminders can serve as a safety net, ensuring that you have ample time to gather necessary documents and make informed decisions about your healthcare.

Here's a list of Medicare Enrollment Periods:

2.3.1 Initial Enrollment Period (IEP)

a. **When**: The seven-month window around your 65th birthday (three months before, the month of, and three months after) when you first become eligible.
b. **Purpose**: This is when you first sign up for Medicare Part A and/or Part B. You can also select a Part D or Medicare Advantage plan during this window.
c. **Example**: If you turn 65 in June, your IEP runs from March 1 – September 30.
d. **Coverage Begins**: The start date for Medicare coverage when you sign up during your Initial Enrollment Period (IEP) depends on the month you enroll:
    - If you enroll anytime in the 3 months before your 65th birthday month, coverage begins on the first day of your birthday month.
    - If you enroll during your birthday month, coverage begins the first day of the following month.
    - If you enroll in the month after your birthday month, coverage begins 2 months after you enroll.
    - If you enroll in the second or third month after your birthday month, coverage begins 3 months after you enroll.

IEP Coverage Begins Example: Birthday is June 10.

Enroll in March, April, or May → Coverage starts June 1.

Enroll in June → Coverage starts July 1.

Enroll in July → Coverage starts September 1.

Enroll in August → Coverage starts November 1.

Enroll in September → Coverage starts December 1.

Enrolling early in your IEP ensures your coverage starts as soon as you are eligible, avoiding any potential gaps in healthcare coverage.

2.3.2 Initial Coverage Election Period (ICEP)

Not to be confused with your IEP and not discussed as often because it only pertains to Medicare eligible folks who enroll in Part B at a different time from Part A and want to also enroll in a Medicare Advantage plan. Remember, you must be enrolled in Part A and B to be eligible for a Medicare Advantage (Part C) plan.

When: The ICEP is the enrollment period for Medicare Advantage (Part C) when you are first eligible for Part C. If you sign up for both Part A and Part B at the same time during your IEP, your ICEP and IEP are the same. If you delay enrolling in Part B (for example, if you keep employer coverage after 65), your Initial Coverage Election Period (ICEP) for Medicare Advantage (Part C) begins three months before your Part B start date and ends the last day of the month before your Part B coverage starts.

Purpose: This is your first chance to enroll in a Medicare Advantage (Part C) plan instead of Original Medicare after enrolling in Part B.

Example: If you turn 65 in June and enroll in both Part A and B at that time, your ICEP is the same as your IEP (March – September). However, if you delay Part B until age 67, your ICEP would begin 3 months before your Part B start date.

Coverage Begins: If you delay Part B until age 67, your Part C coverage will begin the same day your Part B coverage starts, as long as you enroll in the Part C (Medicare Advantage) plan during your ICEP.

ICEP Coverage Begins Example: You turn sixty-seven years old on June 10th and decide to start Part B on June 1st. Your ICEP would run from March 1, 2025 – May 31, 2025. If you enroll in a Medicare Advantage (Part C) plan during your ICEP, coverage will begin June 1, 2025, the same day as your Part B.

In summarizing the last two enrollment periods discussed. The Initial Enrollment Period (IEP) is for signing up for Original Medicare (Parts A & B). Initial Coverage Election Period (ICEP) is for choosing a Medicare Advantage (Part C) plan when first eligible. If you miss your ICEP, you will have to wait until the Annual Election Period (AEP) (Oct 15 - Dec 7) to enroll in a Part C plan.

2.3.3 General Enrollment Period (GEP) and the Medicare Advantage Open Enrollment Period (OEP)

Both GEP and OEP take place during ***the same dates (Jan 1 - Mar 31) but with different purposes.*** I know it can be confusing but think of these enrollment opportunities as a reminder of an important point mentioned earlier in this book—if you're dissatisfied with your current coverage, there are opportunities every year to make changes.

When: January 1 – March 31 each year.

Purpose of the Medicare Advantage OEP: Allows those already in a Medicare Advantage plan to switch to another Medicare Advantage plan or return to Original Medicare. If you are returning to Original Medicare you can enroll in a separate drug plan during this time. You can only make one change during this period, and any changes you make will be effective the first of the month after you submit an application. If you are returning to Original Medicare and joining a separate Medicare drug plan, you do not need to contact your Medicare Advantage Plan to disenroll. The disenrollment will happen automatically when you join the standalone Part D drug plan.

Purpose of the GEP: Allows people to enroll in Medicare Part A and/or Part B if they missed their Initial Enrollment Period and have not experienced a special enrollment opportunity. Late penalties may apply. When you sign up during the General Enrollment Period, your coverage starts the first day of the month after you sign up. If you have Part A coverage and you get Part B for the first time during this period, you can also join a Medicare Advantage Plan.

2.3.4 Annual Enrollment Period (AEP)

When: October 15 – December 7 each year.

Purpose: Review and change your Medicare Advantage (Part C) and/or Prescription Drug Plan (Part D) for the upcoming year. You can join, switch, or drop a Medicare Advantage Plan or Medicare drug plan. The unique feature of this enrollment period is how you can change your mind and make multiple changes between October 15 and Dec 7. The last selection you make will be the one that goes into effect January 1st. This is not something I recommend as a form of plan shopping. This feature is best utilized if you genuinely learn that you have made a mistake, or you felt duped into making an unwanted change. If that happens, rest easy knowing that if you call before December 7 and enroll in a different Medicare Advantage plan, it will automatically replace the unwanted enrollment.

Even if you change your mind after December 7, remember from above, you can switch back to Original Medicare or change to a different Advantage plan between Jan 1 and March 31.

Note: Medigap plan rules are different. Medigap plans are not tied to the Annual Enrollment Period like Medicare Advantage (Part C) or Prescription Drug Plans (Part D). Changes to Medigap plans can be made anytime throughout the year, subject to certain conditions, but medical underwriting may apply. A person cannot typically change Medigap (Medicare Supplement) plans during the Annual Enrollment Period (AEP) between October 15 and December 7.

Summary of What You Can Do During AEP

✓ Switch from Original Medicare (Part A & Part B) to a Medicare Advantage (Part C) plan

✓ Switch from a Medicare Advantage (Part C) plan back to Original Medicare (Parts A & B)

✓ Change from one Medicare Advantage (Part C) plan to another (with or without drug coverage)

✓ Enroll in a Medicare Part D (prescription drug) plan if you don't already have one

✓ Switch from one Medicare Part D plan to another

✓ Drop your Medicare Part D plan completely (though you may face a penalty if you go without creditable drug coverage for too long)

What You CANNOT Do During AEP:

✗ Enroll in a Medigap (Medicare Supplement) plan without medical underwriting (unless you have a guaranteed issue right)

✗ Change from one Medigap plan to another (Medigap changes can be made year-round but may require medical underwriting)

2.4 SPECIAL ENROLLMENT PERIODS (SEPS)

In the future, and for the rest of your days, life events will create Special Enrollment Periods (SEPs) opportunities. The SEP we discussed earlier involved individuals who are still working and covered by an employer's plan, they may decide to delay Medicare enrollment. An SEP kicks in once the employer coverage ends, giving them an additional eight months to enroll. As mentioned earlier, SEPs are also available if you lose coverage due to moving or other qualifying life events. Special Enrollment Periods vary based on certain circumstances. They may allow you to enroll in a Part D or Medicare Advantage when you are outside the standard enrollment periods. There are multiple ways an SEP can help a beneficiary. I'll address the two scenarios we've discussed multiple times so far. The first is when a person misses their initial enrollment period for either Part A or Part B or both. The other scenario is when a beneficiary enrolled in Medicare on time but must make a change to their coverage due to an SEP. SEPs are sometimes forced upon us due to situations out of our control so understanding these scenarios is important.

2.4.1 SEPs for Medicare Parts A & B

Special Enrollment Periods (SEPs) allow people who missed their initial enrollment period for Medicare Parts A and B to enroll without facing late penalties—but only if they qualify for an SEP due to specific life events. Here are some of them:

1. Employer Coverage SEP (Most Common)

If you delayed Medicare because you were covered by an employer-sponsored health plan (yours or your spouse's), you get an 8-month SEP to sign up for Medicare Part A and/or Part B after losing that coverage or leaving the job. This avoids late enrollment penalties.

2. Medicaid SEP

If you lose Medicaid eligibility, you get a 6-month SEP to enroll in Medicare without penalties.

3. Natural Disaster or Emergency SEP

If a FEMA-declared disaster or emergency prevented you from enrolling, you might qualify for a SEP.

4. Misleading Information SEP

If you missed your enrollment period due to incorrect or misleading information from an employer, health plan, or government agency, Medicare may grant you a SEP.

5. Incarceration SEP

If you were incarcerated and missed your enrollment window, you have a 12-month SEP to enroll after release.

6. Foreign Residency SEP

If you were living abroad and didn't enroll in Medicare when first eligible, you may qualify for a SEP upon returning to the U.S.

Important Medicare Part A and B SEP Reminders:

If you do not qualify for a SEP, you must wait for the General Enrollment Period (GEP) (January 1 – March 31) to sign up, and you may face late enrollment penalties. SEPs do not apply to everyone, so it is crucial to check if your situation qualifies.

2.4.2 SEPs That Allow Plan Changes

These SEPs allow beneficiaries to change their Medicare Advantage (Part C) or Part D plans outside of standard enrollment periods. (AEP, OEP and GEP) Each SEP has specific eligibility rules and time limits.

1. **Moving to a New Service Area**: If you move out of your Medicare Advantage or Part D plan's coverage area. Meaning, whenever you change your permanent residence you will have to select coverage for your new location. This SEP begins one month before the move and lasts up to two months after.

2. **Losing Employer, Union, or Other Creditable Coverage:** If you lose health coverage from an employer, union, COBRA, or other creditable coverage (like TRICARE or VA benefits), you can enroll in Medicare or a Medicare Advantage/Part D plan within 2 months of losing coverage.

3. **Gaining/Losing Medicaid or Extra Help**: If you gain or lose Medicaid eligibility or become eligible/ineligible for Extra Help (the low-income subsidy for Part D), you can change plans.

4. **Medicare Savings Program Changes:** If you qualify for a Medicare Savings Program (MSP) or lose eligibility, you can change plans.

5. **Nursing Home or Long-Term Care:** If you move into, reside in, or leave a skilled nursing facility (SNF), long-term care hospital, or rehabilitation center, you can switch plans.

6. Losing or Gaining Institutional Medicaid: If you enter or leave a Medicaid-approved long-term care facility, you can make changes.

7. **Medicare Advantage Plan Termination:** If your Medicare Advantage plan stops offering coverage or is discontinued, you can switch to another plan or return to Original Medicare.

8. Five-Star Plan: If a Medicare Advantage or Part D plan in your area has a 5-star quality rating, you can switch to that plan once per year outside of regular enrollment. This SEP can only be used between Dec. 8 – Nov. 30.

9. Leaving Incarceration: If you were recently released from jail or prison, you can enroll in a Medicare Advantage or Part D plan within 2 months of release.

10. Returning to the USA: If you lived outside the U.S. and return, you can enroll in Medicare Advantage or Part D within 2 months of returning.

11. Disenrolling from Programs Like PACE (Program of All-Inclusive Care for the Elderly): If you leave PACE, you can join a Medicare Advantage or Part D plan within 2 months after leaving PACE.

12. FEMA-Declared Disaster: If you are affected by a natural disaster or emergency, Medicare may grant a SEP to enroll or change plans. The time limits for this SEP vary based on FEMA's declaration.

13. Misleading or Incorrect Plan Information: If you were misled by a plan or employer regarding Medicare enrollment, you can request a SEP to change your plan, but the determination will depend on Medicare's approval.

14. Changes in Special Needs Plan (SNP) Eligibility: If you qualify for, lose eligibility for, or switch Special Needs Plans (SNPs) (for chronic conditions, Medicaid, or institutionalized care), you can switch plans. This SEP will apply anytime you qualify or within 3 months after losing eligibility.

2.5 TRANSITION FROM EMPLOYER INSURANCE

Transitioning from employer insurance to Medicare is like stepping into a new chapter of healthcare coverage, requiring thoughtful coordination and clear communication. As you approach this change, it's critical to have an action plan that addresses the end of your employer-provided insurance and the initiation of your Medicare coverage. Start by reviewing the details of your current plan and understanding when your coverage will terminate. Typically, employer plans remain active until the last day of the month your employment ends, but this can vary based on your company's policies. Confirming these specifics with your HR department to avoid surprises is essential. Open a dialogue with your HR representative early, as they can provide critical information and documentation needed for a smooth transition. They also assist in verifying any benefits that may extend beyond your employment, such as retiree health benefits, which can be crucial in bridging any potential gaps in coverage.

COBRA, the Consolidated Omnibus Budget Reconciliation Act, often enters the conversation during this transition. COBRA allows you to continue your employer health insurance for a limited time after leaving your job, but navigating its implications alongside Medicare requires careful consideration. While COBRA coverage may seem like a convenient safety net, it is important to note that it does not count as creditable coverage for Medicare. If you delay enrolling in Medicare because you have COBRA, then you could face late enrollment penalties. Timing is everything here; for most, enrolling in Medicare when first eligible is advisable to avoid complications and unnecessary expenses. If you find yourself with COBRA coverage, weigh your options carefully. Consider your healthcare needs, costs, and any potential penalties. Consulting with a Medicare expert or advisor can provide clarity and help you make informed decisions tailored to your situation.

Ensuring a seamless transition is paramount to maintaining continuous healthcare coverage. Avoiding gaps is not just about covering medical services; it is also about peace of mind and knowing that you can access care when needed. To achieve this, plan by lining up your Medicare start date with the end of your employer insurance. Double check that your Medicare coverage is active before your employer plan ends. This requires timely enrollment in Medicare Part A and Part B, typically during your Initial Enrollment Period if you are leaving work around age 65. Prescription drug coverage is another critical aspect to consider. If you are taking medications, ensure no Part D coverage lapses. Evaluate your options for drug plans under Medicare and enroll as needed to maintain uninterrupted prescription access.

2.5.1 Real Example: Susan

One of my clients, Susan, had already planned to retire at 65 when we first spoke. Her birthday month was August. She enrolled online into Medicare Parts A and B using ssa.gov in May for a start date of August 1. I remember her saying she enrolled in Parts A and B over Mother's Day weekend as a gift to herself. Her official Medicare Health Insurance card arrived over the summer, showing the Effective Dates for A and B as August 1. That gave her the confidence to give her employer a retirement date of August 20. She knew the employer plan would remain in effect until August 31, creating a one month overlap. She explained how the one month overlap in health insurance coverage, and having her Medicare card in hand, gave her peace of mind. This was her strategy, and it made total sense to me.

Also, her plan demonstrated a common retirement scenario: She did not want to leave the company until she was on Medicare. Although the ACA marketplace allows anyone to find medical coverage when they are 64 years old or younger if they lose employer coverage this was the scenario Susan wanted to avoid. She had a high-salaried job, enrolling in a marketplace medical plan or using COBRA would have been expensive compared to Medicare. So, all the foundational work was done when she called me in July. We only had to discuss how she wanted to get her drug coverage. Susan lived in a service area that offered excellent Medicare Advantage plans by a few top insurance companies. Also, her doctor's office accepted many Medicare Advantage PPO plans, and a few of her friends were extremely happy with their Part C coverage. After our lengthy discussion about key benefits and drug copays, she confidently picked a plan, and we completed her enrollment over the phone for a start date of August 1.

3

REVIEW OF MEDICARE FUNDAMENTALS

Up to this point, we have explored a significant amount of information in a short span. To ensure clarity and reinforce key concepts, this section serves as a final comprehensive primer on your Medicare options. It provides a structured review of previously discussed topics while incorporating additional details to enhance your understanding.

3.1 ORIGINAL MEDICARE VS. MEDICARE ADVANTAGE

Choosing between Original Medicare and Medicare Advantage is a decision that many find pivotal, and rightly so. Each option has benefits and potential drawbacks, making this choice highly personal. Original Medicare, consisting of Part A and Part B, offers freedom many find appealing. It allows you to visit any doctor or hospital in the US that accepts Medicare without needing referrals to see specialists. This flexibility can be particularly beneficial if you have a trusted network of healthcare providers, or if you travel frequently and want the assurance that you can access medical care wherever you are. However, it's important to remember that Original Medicare doesn't cover everything; expenses like routine vision and dental care are not included, and you'll typically pay 20% of the Medicare-approved amount for Part B services after meeting your deductible (U.S. Centers for Medicare and Medicaid Services, n.d.). This is why so many people enroll in a Medigap plan, also called a Supplement plan. These plans will have an additional monthly premium on top of the $185 Part B premium.

On the other hand, Medicare Advantage, also known as Part C, bundles together Parts A and B, often including Part D for prescription drug coverage. Private companies approved by Medicare offer these plans, usually with additional benefits like vision, dental, and gym memberships. However, the trade-off is that you generally must use the plan's network of doctors and hospitals, which can limit your choices. Some plans require referrals to see specialists, and prior authorization for certain services might be needed. Financially, Medicare Advantage plans can be attractive because they have a yearly limit on out-of-pocket expenses for covered services. Once you reach this limit, you pay nothing for covered services for the rest of the year, providing a financial safety net that Original Medicare lacks.

When considering cost implications, Medicare Advantage plans might offer lower or even $0 premiums in some areas but may include additional costs depending on your services. On the flip side, if you choose Original Medicare, then you'll probably want to enroll in a Medigap policy to help cover out-of-pocket expenses like deductibles and coinsurance. Medigap can reduce the unpredictability of medical costs, but it does come with an additional premium. This balance between predictable costs and flexibility is a central consideration in your decision-making process.

Lifestyle and health needs are crucial in determining which Medicare option suits you best. Original Medicare might be the way to go if you value the ability to travel without worrying about network restrictions. However, if managing a chronic condition with comprehensive coverage is your priority, then the all-inclusive nature of Medicare Advantage—with its additional benefits—could be more appealing. The choice often boils down to how you weigh the importance of flexibility against potential savings and added benefits.

Writing things down helps many of my clients with these decisions. List your healthcare priorities, such as preferred doctors, potential travel plans, and specific health needs, like prescription coverage or additional services. A summary of differences is also included below for ease of reference (U.S. Centers for Medicare and Medicaid Services, n.d.):

3.1.1 Original Medicare Summary

- Coverage provided by the Federal Government
- Includes Part A (Hospital Insurance) & Part B (Medical Insurance)
- No Network Restrictions – Beneficiaries can usually see any doctor or specialist in the U.S. who accepts Medicare, without referrals.
- Out-of-Pocket Costs to include deductibles, copayments, and coinsurance, with no annual out-of-pocket limit unless combined with supplemental coverage (Medigap).

- Prescription Drugs Not Included – Requires a separate Part D plan.
- Private Medigap policies can help cover cost gaps like deductibles and coinsurance.

3.1.2 Medicare Advantage (Part C) Summary

- Plan coverage is issued by private insurers.
- It is referred to as Part C.
- It must provide at least the same coverage as Parts A and B.
- It does cap out-of-pocket expenses, and it may include drug coverage (Part D).
- It usually requires services to be done by network providers.
- The plan types include PPO, HMO, HMO-POS, MSA, PFFS, and SNP

3.1.3 Real Example: Mr. & Mrs. Albright

Sometimes, the need to make a change is evident. Medigap monthly premiums increase yearly in some instances. I estimate it's the biggest reason many people switch from Original Medicare to Medicare Advantage. I recently helped the Albrights, a couple living in New Jersey outside New York City. They were upset because their monthly supplement and drug plan premiums increased again. The total for each of them was nearly $450 every month. That's $900/month for Medicare coverage for a two-person household. They were struggling financially like so many seniors today, but they were grateful for their good health. Much to my chagrin, they explained how they rarely see doctors out of fear of more medical expenses. We worked together and found a Medicare Advantage PPO plan widely accepted in their service area with a $0 monthly premium. The plan includes prescription drug coverage and dental, hearing, and vision allowances. We discussed the potential out-of-pocket cost scenarios if they switched to Medicare Advantage. Still, they both gleefully enrolled in the Part C plan. Their story is just one example of why you may want to make changes in the future. This household is now saving $900/month. Most importantly, they now understand the importance and affordability of participating in preventive care with their Primary Care Physician every year--by law, most preventive services have a $0 copay.

3.2 SUPPLEMENT PLANS: FILLING THE GAPS IN YOUR COVERAGE

As a reminder to avoid confusion, the terms Medigap and Supplement are used interchangeably in the realm of Original Medicare. These plans are designed to cover extra costs that Original Medicare doesn't, like copayments, coinsurance, and deductibles. Think of Medigap as the friend who picks up the tab when you've forgotten your wallet. These plans are standardized across most states, meaning Plan G in one state offers the same benefits as Plan G in another. This standardization simplifies the process, making it easier to compare plans and find one that fits your needs without surprises. Medigap offers peace of mind by covering out-of-pocket costs, ensuring unexpected expenses don't throw your budget off balance.

Timing is crucial when it comes to enrolling in a Medigap plan. The best time to sign up is during your Medigap Open Enrollment Period. This six-month period starts when you turn 65 and are enrolled in Medicare Part B. During this time, you can buy any Medigap policy sold in your state, regardless of your health conditions. If you miss this window, then you might face higher premiums or even be denied coverage based on health issues later. It's a limited time offer that guarantees you the best deal. Outside of this period, insurance companies can use medical underwriting, which means they can consider your health status when deciding whether to sell you a policy and at what price.

Medigap plans come in several varieties, with Plans F, G, and N being some of the most popular:

- Plan F is known for its comprehensive coverage, paying for nearly all out-of-pocket costs, but it's only available to those eligible for Medicare before 2020.
- Plan G is similar, but it doesn't cover the Part B deductible.
- Plan N, on the other hand, offers lower premiums in exchange for some copayments for office and emergency room visits.

If you're considering a high-deductible plan, note that it may offer lower premiums, but require you to pay a higher deductible before coverage kicks in. Each plan provides a different balance of premiums and out-of-pocket costs, allowing you to choose based on your financial situation and healthcare needs.

A common misconception about Medigap is that it covers everything under the sun. However, it's essential to know that Medigap doesn't cover prescription drugs. For that, you'll need a separate Part D plan. Also, while Medigap can cover foreign travel emergencies up to plan limits, it's not designed for comprehensive international coverage. Understanding these limits helps you plan effectively, ensuring you're not caught off guard by unexpected expenses.

Medigap plans offer a tailored approach to healthcare coverage, picking up where Original Medicare leaves off. You can build a robust healthcare strategy by understanding how these plans work and aligning them with your needs. The key is to assess your situation, consider your health status and financial goals, and choose a plan that provides the right level of support. With Medigap, you're not just filling gaps, but also building a safety net that can catch you when unexpected healthcare costs arise.

3.3 UNDERSTANDING PRESCRIPTION DRUG COVERAGE WITH PART D

Navigating the landscape of Medicare Part D can feel like stepping into a pharmacy with endless aisles of choices. Understanding how these plans work is crucial to ensure your medications are covered without breaking the bank. Part D plans are structured around formularies, which are essentially lists of covered drugs. Each insurance company has its own formulary that categorizes the medications into **tiers.** These tiers categorize drugs based on factors like cost and brand status, influencing the copayments or coinsurance amounts you pay.

While **4-tier formularies are prevalent**, some plans may offer **more complex structures**, such as **5 or 6 tiers**, to provide a broader range of cost-sharing options. The specific tier structure can vary by plan and insurer.

The tier system can influence how much you pay for each medication. Generally, lower-tier drugs like generics cost less, while higher-tier drugs—often brand-name medications—come with steeper price tags. Checking the formulary of any plan you consider is vital. It ensures that your necessary prescriptions are covered and can help avoid unexpected costs.

Enrolling in a Part D plan does not have to be a stressor. If you are working with a licensed agent they will enter all your prescription information into the secure enrollment system and provide you with solid estimates of your drug costs for any given plan.

This section is to give you a rough idea of what Part D plans will cost. According to CMS.gov, in 2025, the average monthly premium for Medicare Part D prescription drug plans throughout the US is projected to be **$46.50**, a decrease from $53.95 in 2024. However, as we discussed earlier, actual premiums can differ depending on the region and the specific plans available.

Additionally, in 2025, a significant change is the implementation of a **$2,000 cap on out-of-pocket prescription drug costs** for Part D enrollees which has already started making a huge difference in many American households.

This may sound strange but sometimes people struggle to hear good news regarding the lowering of Part D monthly premiums.

3.3.1 Real Example: Julie

Julie, a retiree who is relatively healthy and very budget-conscious, called me sounding worried. She just received a notice from her Part D insurance company that her plan's monthly premium would be lowering to $17/month starting in January 2025. "Omg, how can that be? What's wrong here? Will my meds still be covered?" She was really concerned. I said, "It sounds like great news, but let's double check." I went to that company's website and entered all her meds to compare estimated copays for 2025. Sure enough, this was a good news scenario. That was the company's newly published plan pricing, and her copays stayed the same. My challenge was to explain that I didn't know exactly why the carrier was able to lower the monthly premium for her Part D plan and that sometimes all we have to do is remain open to hearing good news.

3.3.2 The Medicare Prescription Payment Plan (M3P)

Effective January 1, 2025, M3P is a new option designed to help Medicare beneficiaries manage their out-of-pocket prescription drug costs by spreading payments throughout the year (U.S. Centers for Medicare and Medicaid Services, n.d.).

How M3P Works:

- **Monthly Payments:** Instead of paying the full cost of your medications at the pharmacy, you'll receive a monthly bill from your Medicare drug plan or Medicare Advantage Plan with drug coverage. This bill will include the amount you owe for any prescriptions filled during the month, divided by the months remaining in the year.
- **No Upfront Payments at Pharmacy:** You won't pay the pharmacy directly when you fill a prescription. Your plan will cover the cost, and you'll reimburse them through your monthly payments.
- **Annual Out-of-pocket Cap:** Regardless of your monthly payments, your total out-of-pocket prescription drug costs will not exceed $2,000 in 2025. This cap applies to all Medicare beneficiaries, even if you don't participate in M3P.

M3P is particularly beneficial for individuals who have high prescription drug costs early in the year and/or they take medications with significant out-of-pocket expenses. By enrolling in M3P, you can avoid large upfront payments and manage your expenses more evenly throughout the year. You can opt into M3P at any time during the year by contacting your Medicare drug plan or Medicare Advantage Plan with drug coverage. Enrolling early in the year is advisable to maximize the benefit of spreading payments over more months. Participating in M3P is free; no extra fees or interest charges exist. An important note about **payment responsibility:** While M3P helps manage payment timing, it doesn't reduce the total amount you owe for your medications. You'll still be responsible for the full cost, but the payment schedule is more manageable.

You can refer to the official Medicare resources on the Prescription Payment Plan for more detailed information.

3.4 THE IMPORTANCE OF PREVENTIVE SERVICES IN MEDICARE

Imagine setting out on a morning walk—the sun warming your face, the air crisp and refreshing. Just as you walk to maintain your physical health, Medicare also offers preventive services to keep you healthy in the long run. These services are designed to catch potential health issues early, often before symptoms even appear, allowing for more manageable treatments and better outcomes. Medicare covers a range of preventive services at no cost to you. This includes annual wellness visits, which provide an opportunity to assess your health and update your prevention plan. During these visits, you and your doctor can discuss your current health status and concerns, ensuring that any emerging issues are addressed promptly.

Screenings for diabetes, cancer, and cardiovascular disease are also part of Medicare's preventive services. These tests are vital because they help detect diseases in their earliest stages when they are most treatable. Regular screenings can differentiate between a minor health hiccup and a major medical challenge. For instance, diabetes screenings can catch elevated blood sugar levels before they develop into full-blown diabetes, allowing you to take preventive actions. Meanwhile, cancer screenings, such as mammograms or colonoscopies, can identify abnormal growths early, increasing treatment success rates. These services safeguard your health and potentially reduce long-term healthcare costs.

In addition to screenings, Medicare covers vaccinations for illnesses like influenza and pneumonia. These vaccinations are crucial, especially as we age, because they help protect against severe illness. Vaccinating reduces your risk of catching and spreading these diseases to others.

Another valuable preventive service is bone mass measurement, which helps detect osteoporosis early. This condition can lead to fractures and significant mobility issues, so early detection and treatment are essential for maintaining independence and quality of life. These preventive measures are about more than just avoiding illness; they enable you to live your best life, filled with vitality and well-being.

Proactive health management involves more than just attending appointments; it's about building a preventive care schedule that you adhere to regularly. This schedule should include all the screenings and vaccinations recommended for your age and health status. A plan helps ensure you don't miss crucial preventive care opportunities. Maintaining open communication with your healthcare provider about available screenings and tests is vital. They can guide you in understanding which services are most relevant to your health profile and ensure you stay on top of necessary preventive measures. This proactive approach empowers you to take control of your health, reducing the likelihood of unexpected medical issues and enhancing your overall quality of life.

If you need another good reason to become established with a Primary Care practice, consider this—**your money**! Staying on top of your healthcare is the best way to avoid unnecessary out-of-pocket medical expenses.

The annual preventive screenings could prevent surgeries, hospital stays, and expensive medications. Early detection is everything nowadays. If you struggle with making medical appointments, please ask someone for assistance.

As we conclude this chapter, I hope you'll reflect on how preventive services are crucial to your medical condition. They prevent illness and promote long-term health and independence; keeping up with them can save your life.

3.4.1 Real Example: Margaret

Colorectal cancer is one of the most treatable forms of cancer, yet it is a leading cause of cancer-related deaths in the United States, with an estimated 53,000 deaths in 2024 (American Cancer Society, n.d.). A significant portion of these deaths occur among individuals who never did a screening. Margaret's family had a well-known medical history of colon cancer. Her father died of it decades ago as did another relative. Margaret's sister, per her doctor's orders, scheduled a colonoscopy every three years during which the gastroenterologist would sometimes remove polyps. Margaret never scheduled a colonoscopy and even lied to friends and family when they pressed her for reassurances that she had. Tragically, Margaret died at 64 years old from colon cancer. Her older sister is still alive and well.

4

AVOIDING PITFALLS AND MISCONCEPTIONS

Picture yourself standing in a bustling marketplace, surrounded by the hum of conversation and the aroma of fresh produce. You hear snippets of advice about Medicare from passing strangers—some of it good, some of it misleading. In this vibrant scene, it's easy to see how misconceptions about Medicare can spread quickly. Much like overhearing a rumor in a crowd, misinformation about Medicare can soon lead to confusion. That's why we're here: to debunk some of the most common myths that might be causing you unnecessary worry.

4.1 MEDICARE MISCONCEPTIONS

4.1.2 Misconception: Long-term Care

A common misunderstanding involves long-term care. Many people assume that Medicare will cover the cost of extended stays in nursing homes or long-term care facilities, but this is not the case. While Medicare offers limited coverage for short-term nursing care In Skilled Nursing facilities following a hospital stay, it does not provide long-term custodial care, including assistance with daily activities like bathing, dressing, and eating. This is a critical distinction, as long-term care can be a significant expense for many seniors. By understanding this limitation, you can consider other options, such as long-term care insurance or Medicaid, which may offer broader coverage for these needs.

4.1.3 Misconception: Eligibility

Misunderstandings about Medicare eligibility are common, with many believing that all seniors automatically receive Medicare once they reach 65. The truth is that automatic enrollment only occurs if you are already receiving Social Security benefits. If not, you must enroll yourself to avoid late penalties. Furthermore, eligibility hinges on work credits—typically, you need 40 credits, or approximately 10 years of work, to qualify for premium-free Part A. Those without enough work history may have to pay a premium for Part A, which emphasizes the importance of verifying your eligibility status to avoid unwelcome surprises.

4.1.4 Misconception: Parts A and B are Enough

There's also confusion surrounding the role of supplemental insurance. Many people mistakenly believe that Original Medicare alone will suffice, but these supplemental plans, also known as medigap plans, can significantly enhance your coverage. Medigap policies help cover out-of-pocket expenses that Original Medicare does not, such as deductibles and copayments. On the other hand, Medicare Advantage plans offer an alternative to Original Medicare, often bundling Part A, Part B, and usually Part D, along with additional benefits like routine hearing, vision and dental care. Relying solely on Medicare Parts A and B may leave you exposed to significant out-of-pocket costs, as they do not cover prescription drugs, routine dental or vision care, and have no cap on annual expenses. To ensure comprehensive coverage and financial protection, it's essential to consider additional options such as a Medicare Supplement (Medigap) plan or a Medicare Advantage plan with built-in benefits.

4.1.5 Misconception: Drugs

Prescription drug coverage is another area rife with confusion. Medicare Part D provides coverage for prescription medications, but not all drugs are automatically covered. Each Part D plan has its formulary, or a list of drugs it covers, which is divided into tiers affecting your out-of-pocket costs. Reviewing these formularies is essential to ensure your medications are included so you can anticipate potential costs. This proactive approach helps you avoid the frustration of finding out too late that a necessary medication isn't covered or is more expensive than expected.

4.1.6 Test Your Knowledge

Test your knowledge with this short quiz to reinforce what you've learned about Medicare misconceptions. Give each statement a True or False answer.

1. Medicare covers all medical expenses, including dental and vision care.
2. All seniors automatically receive Medicare at age 65, regardless of work history.
3. Medigap and Medicare Advantage plans serve the same purpose and offer identical coverage.
4. Irrespective of the plan, every prescription drug is covered under Medicare Part D.

Answers: 1. False, 2. False, 3. False, 4. False.

Understanding your plan options is a crucial step in the enrollment process. Many people rush into choosing a plan without thoroughly researching the differences, leading to dissatisfaction and unexpected costs. Before enrolling, take the time to compare available plans, considering factors like coverage, costs, and provider networks.

You don't have to navigate this research alone. Working with a licensed agent can simplify the process, providing you with multiple coverage options quickly and efficiently—whether over the phone or in person. To further empower clients, I can email them a digital guidebook summarizing the top two or three plans discussed, allowing them to analyze their options at their own pace. Once they've made a decision, they can conveniently enroll on their own by clicking an **Enroll** button, ensuring a seamless and stress-free experience.

There are also online tools that offer side-by-side comparisons, allowing you to see the benefits and drawbacks of each plan. These can be found on most carrier websites and Medicare.gov. This analysis helps you select a plan that aligns with your healthcare needs and financial situation, preventing unpleasant surprises. Knowledge is power, and in the context of Medicare, it empowers you to make timely and informed decisions to give you peace of mind.

4.1.7 Real Example: Mary

Mary, a retiree who missed her Part B enrollment deadline, thought she didn't need Part B because she was healthy and rarely visited the doctor. However, when she suffered an unexpected injury, the absence of Part B left her facing significant out-of-pocket costs. The penalty she incurred for late enrollment added to her financial burden, which could have been avoided with timely enrollment when she first became eligible.

4.1.8 Real Example: Jim

Jim chose a Medicare Advantage HMO plan without understanding its network restrictions. Jim loved traveling to see his grandchildren but soon found that his plan didn't cover out-of-network providers, limiting his healthcare options when away from home. These scenarios highlight the importance of understanding the full scope of your Medicare plan and its potential implications on your lifestyle.

4.2 NO NEED TO UNDERSTAND THE DONUT HOLE

Great news! You do not need to understand the donut hole because it no longer exists. If you have experienced it, you know what I'm talking about. This gap often meant that folks would be going through the calendar year just fine, paying reasonable copays for their meds. Suddenly, usually sometime between September and December, after spending a certain amount on prescriptions, their out-of-pocket costs would skyrocket. It was a perplexing and stressful situation, causing many to dread the latter months of the year when these costs typically surged.

However, significant legislative changes have fixed this problem, effectively closing the donut hole starting in 2025. This means you no longer have to brace yourself for a sudden financial burden each fall, allowing for a more manageable and predictable approach to handling prescription drug costs. This change is such a welcome relief for millions. Eliminating the donut hole marks a pivotal shift that allows you to plan and manage your medication expenses more effectively, reducing stress and lifting the fear of financial ruin.

As a result, the new Medicare Part D structure allows you to approach prescription drug planning with newfound clarity and confidence.

4.3 COST MANAGEMENT STRATEGIES

Of course everyone would love to do careful financial planning, as healthcare expenses can be unpredictable. This subject is a very sensitive one for many people I've assisted across 26 states. Most seniors think they don't have enough money to do a lot of financial planning. They receive a Social Security or other retirement income and live on a fixed budget. I completely understand. Most seniors in the US have never worked with a financial planner. However, it's never too late to create and analyze a monthly budget. All the experts tell us we must know exactly what is going out so we can find ways to save.

4.3.1 Budgeting

This is not easy for everyone, but consider creating a budget for monthly premiums, regular medications, and potential unexpected medical expenses. This approach can help you prepare for the routine and the unpredictable, ensuring you have a financial cushion should your health needs change. This will be easier once you know your monthly premiums and drug copays. Now that you understand the importance of your Medicare premiums, you'll find ways to make these expenditures a top priority.

4.3.2 Preventive Services

One effective strategy to manage and reduce healthcare expenses is to use Medicare's preventive services fully. These services can help you catch potential health issues early, often before they become more serious and costly. For instance, routine screenings and vaccinations are designed to keep you healthy, reducing the likelihood of needing more extensive medical interventions. By prioritizing preventive care, you maintain better health and save money by avoiding the high costs of untreated conditions. Additionally, it's worth exploring supplemental insurance options if you can afford it. Medigap policies can cover expenses that Original Medicare doesn't, such as copayments and deductibles.

4.3.3 Medicare Advantage Plans

Medicare Advantage plans are highly recommended for folks desperately strapped for monthly income. They often have a $0 monthly premium, as well as Dental, Vision, and Hearing allowances. Some Medicare Advantage plans offer a Part B Giveback, which is a contribution to the $185 Part B monthly premium we all pay. It shows up as a raise in your monthly Social Security check if you are paying the Part B premium; many seniors need that money for groceries every month.

4.3.4 Assistance Programs

There are also several assistance programs designed to help with Medicare costs. Medicare Savings Programs can assist with paying Part A and Part B premiums and other expenses like deductibles and copayments. If you have limited income and resources, these programs can be a lifeline, easing the financial burden.

Similarly, the Extra Help program offered through the Social Security Administration is available for those who need assistance with out-of-pocket prescription drug costs. Many Medicare members qualify for these savings, but don't know it. You must apply online or stop by your local Social Security office. This program can significantly reduce the cost of medications, ensuring you can afford the drugs you need without sacrificing other essentials. In 2024 approximately 3 million Medicare Part D enrollees received premium and cost-sharing assistance through the Extra Help program.

A Medicare beneficiary receiving Extra Help (Low-Income Subsidy for Part D) typically does not need to reapply every year, but their eligibility is reviewed annually.

Automatic Renewal happens when a beneficiary's financial situation remains the same; in this best case scenario you will continue receiving Extra Help without needing to reapply.

Annual Redetermination (Late Summer to Fall) is when Medicare, Medicaid, or the Social Security Administration (SSA) determines that a beneficiary's financial situation has changed. In this scenario you may receive a redetermination notice requiring you to provide updated income and asset information.

Reapplication is required when you are not automatically renewed. If a beneficiary loses eligibility due to income or resource changes, they will need to reapply.

When in doubt, when should a beneficiary reapply? If they receive a notice from SSA stating they no longer automatically qualify.

How to Reapply for Extra Help: There are several options.

Apply online at www.ssa.gov/extrahelp

Call Social Security at 1-800-772-1213

Visit a local Social Security office

Get assistance from SHIP (State Health Insurance Assistance Program)

4.3.5 Real Example: Harold

Harold is a retiree who successfully managed his Medicare expenses using a few different resources. He explained that he wasn't a super strict budgeter in the past, but now that he has more time, he pays close attention to his healthcare expenses and tries to set aside $50 every month in anticipation of out-of-pocket costs. He selected a Medigap plan with a tolerable monthly premium of $134/month and a standalone Part D plan for $34/month. Harold made it a point to attend regular health check-ups which have helped him stay on top of his health and avoid costly medical treatments. He applied and qualified for Extra Help with his prescription drug costs, which ended up paying his Part D premium and drug copays. This proactive approach allowed Harold to maintain his financial security while meeting his healthcare needs.

4.3.6 Real Example: Bob

When Bob and I first spoke, his growing prescription drug costs were becoming unmanageable. He insisted that he would never qualify for assistance because he owned his home. I explained how that is not true for some assistance programs. I urged him to visit his local Social Security office and apply for the Extra Help program. When we spoke again, he indicated that he had received a letter stating he qualified for Extra Help, which will now pay his Part D monthly premium and prescription copays. I could hear the relief in this voice, but he didn't understand how it would work. More great news: He doesn't have to do anything differently; simply continue picking up his meds at the pharmacy per his usual routine. Like most Medicare financial transactions, it happens automatically in the system. Some years he receives a letter asking him to reapply. The letter misleads people. It doesn't mean he's been kicked out of the Extra Help program; rather, they simply need him to reapply to ensure he still requires assistance.

4.3.7 Real Example: Darlene

Darlene has been a member of Medicare Advantage plans since she turned 65. She lives in a Florida county where these plans are widely accepted and has never had a problem with her doctors and specialists accepting her Advantage PPO plan. This approach has always worked for her because of the $0 monthly premium and no additional premium for a drug plan. She also receives a Part B Giveback of $85 monthly, which she puts towards expensive dental work and designer eyeglasses. Her Advantage plan has a Dental and Vision allowance, which is a big help, but it's usually insufficient to cover everything. She's aware that she may incur out-of-pocket bills for unexpected ailments and hospital stays, but she hasn't experienced any financial issues yet. Last year, she had an emergency gallbladder removal, which is a costly surgery, and she didn't pay a single penny out of pocket.

In summarizing cost management strategies, the best advice I can leave with you is that managing your Medicare expenses is a dynamic process that requires attention and, most importantly, the gumption to ask for assistance. Every state has programs designed to help seniors with medical expenses—you just have to reach out. These programs exist specifically to support you, and there's no shame in using them. This isn't charity; most of these benefits are funded by the tax dollars you've paid over the years. Sure, there might be a little paperwork involved, but if I told you these programs could save you hundreds, maybe even thousands of dollars each year, wouldn't it be worth the effort? Maybe even worth a trip to your local Social Security office? As you navigate this process, remember—these resources are tools to help you live more comfortably and with greater peace of mind, knowing your healthcare costs are under control.

4.4 ACTUAL COST ESTIMATES

Darlene's story illustrates why you won't have medical bills for certain expensive scenarios. Medicare covers gallbladder, appendix, hernia, fracture repair, valve replacement, and many other essential surgeries based on the medical necessity and criteria set by the program. Here's a quick rundown on how Medicare decides what gets covered.

4.4.1 Medical Necessity

I use Darlene's emergency gallbladder removal as an example because it helps illustrate the types of surgeries covered. This surgery often addresses acute conditions like gallbladder inflammation (cholecystitis), gallstones blocking bile flow, or severe infection. These conditions are life-threatening if not treated immediately, qualifying them as medically necessary. Medicare does not cover surgeries unless deemed medically necessary to treat a specific illness, injury, or condition.

4.4.2 Urgency and Risk

Emergency surgeries, like gallbladder removal, are typically covered because they address acute, high-risk situations where delaying treatment could lead to severe complications, organ failure, or death.

Non-emergency or elective surgeries may not carry the same immediate risks, so they may not qualify for Medicare coverage unless supported by a clear medical need.

4.4.3 Type of Surgery

Medicare covers surgeries for specific illnesses or injuries, including emergency procedures, surgeries to address chronic conditions, and some preventive procedures. Examples include appendectomies, hernia repairs, or hip replacements (if medically justified). Surgeries for aesthetic or lifestyle purposes (e.g., cosmetic surgery,) are not covered.

4.4.4 Medicare Policy and Guidelines

Medicare operates under strict guidelines, requiring surgeries to be performed in a certified facility. Surgeries must be ordered by a Medicare-participating provider, and they must be supported by documentation showing the procedure is necessary for the patient's health or to prevent further harm. Fortunately, it's standard procedure nowadays for providers to request prior authorization before performing anything but routine care.

4.4.5 Supplement (Medigap) Plan Premiums

Within the scope of this book, it's impossible to provide even estimates of Medigap monthly premiums throughout the US because prices vary significantly based on several key factors, including:

- Location – Premiums differ by state and ZIP code due to regional healthcare costs and insurer competition.
- Age & Pricing Method – Insurers use community-rated, issue-age-rated, or attained-age-rated pricing, which affects costs differently.
- Gender & Tobacco Use – Some insurers charge higher premiums for men or smokers.
- Insurance Provider – Different private insurers set their own rates, leading to wide cost variations.
- Discounts & Underwriting – Some insurers offer household discounts, while others may charge higher rates if you enroll outside your Medigap Open Enrollment Period.

Because of these variables, it's important to know how to find accurate Medigap premium prices for the wide variety of options. You can check with insurers directly for your specific location and personal circumstances or work with a licensed agent who can also look up plan prices. There's also Medicare's Plan Finder tool to compare prices in your area and find exact costs. For Community-Rated Plans, everyone pays the same rate regardless of age. There are also Issue-Age Rated Plans, for which premiums are based on your age at enrollment. Lastly, there are Attained-Age Rated Plans, where the premiums increase as you age. Yes, the Supplement Plan menu can be complicated depending on your location. This paragraph highlights why so many people enjoy Medicare Advantage plans: They're easy to understand especially if you've been on an HMO or PPO in the past.

5

MEETING YOUR UNIQUE NEEDS

Choosing the right Medicare plan starts with a thoughtful assessment of your healthcare needs. Consider the medical services you frequently use. Do you regularly visit a particular specialist or require ongoing physical therapy? Identifying these patterns in your healthcare usage is crucial. Your current health status is essential, but considering potential changes is also wise. Think about your family history and any conditions that might arise. Preparing for these possibilities can help you choose a plan that provides comprehensive coverage, allowing you to focus on maintaining your health and well-being without worry. This proactive approach ensures that your Medicare plan reflects your healthcare needs, providing peace of mind and stability.

Geographic location plays a significant role in determining your Medicare plans. As previously mentioned, location is everything—where you live influences your Medicare choices. Plan availability can vary widely from state to state, and even within regions. Some areas offer many options, while others might have limited choices. This variability can affect the plans you can choose and your access to network providers. For instance, you might face challenges finding providers within your plan's network if you reside in a rural area. Conversely, urban areas often have a wider range of in-network providers, offering more flexibility in choosing healthcare services. Understanding how your location impacts your options is essential in selecting a plan that meets your needs.

Your lifestyle and travel habits also warrant consideration when choosing a Medicare plan. If you enjoy traveling frequently or living part-time in different states, then you'll want a plan that accommodates this mobility. Some plans offer national networks, providing coverage across state lines that is ideal for those who move around often. Others might have more localized networks, requiring careful coordination to ensure coverage when traveling. Evaluate how these aspects fit into your lifestyle. This consideration ensures that your healthcare remains seamless and uninterrupted, regardless of where life takes you. It's about aligning your Medicare coverage with your circumstances, making sure you have the flexibility and support you need.

Several tools are available to assist in evaluating and comparing plan options. Online comparison tools are handy, allowing you to input your preferences and healthcare needs to see which plans align best with your criteria. These tools can help you weigh costs, coverage, and provider networks, providing a clear picture of your options. Additionally, I recommend working with a licensed Medicare agent like me for personalized guidance. These professionals can provide insights tailored to your unique situation, helping you easily navigate the complexities of Medicare. Access to these resources empowers you to make informed decisions, ensuring your Medicare plan perfectly fits your needs.

5.1 MEDICARE AND VETERANS

For some veterans, the timing of integrating VA benefits with Medicare also requires attention, and there are a wide variety of scenarios. Not all veterans use the Department of Veteran Affairs (the VA) for their medical care. For example, I'm a veteran who has never used VA care since I left the Air Force. I've been a civilian for decades and have always had medical coverage through my employer or my husband's employment. It was easier for me to keep it simple and manage the entire family's medical care with one civilian plan.

The Department of Veterans Affairs (VA) estimates that more than half of U.S. veterans do not regularly rely on VA healthcare services (U.S. Department of Veteran Affairs, n.d.). One of the reasons is that not all veterans qualify for VA healthcare. Service-connected disability ratings, income levels, and other criteria determine eligibility. Some veterans may not apply because they assume they are ineligible or are unaware of their benefits. Also, VA facilities may not be conveniently located, making access difficult for veterans in rural or underserved areas. Lastly, veterans may have private or employer-sponsored insurance and prefer to use their existing doctors and networks, similar to my scenario.

However, all veterans are encouraged to register for Medicare at 65 years old, and everything outlined in this book applies to them. Please also note: From now on in this chapter, when I use the term veteran, it's only referring to those who routinely receive healthcare through the Department of Veterans Affairs (VA).

5.1.1 Are Veterans Required to Enroll in Medicare?

Again, this section is for veterans who routinely receive healthcare and meds from the VA. You are not technically nor legally required to register for Medicare. Still, it is highly recommended that you register for Parts A and B as soon as you are eligible, especially Part A, because it will not cost you anything.

Here's why this is so strongly recommended: Your VA medical care will work in coordination with Medicare. VA hospitals and clinics offer specialized care, often providing services not covered by Medicare. Medicare cannot pay for care received at VA facilities but covers care at non-VA facilities. Therefore, having Medicare allows veterans to access care outside the VA system, including emergency care, specialists, and non-VA hospitals. This dual coverage can help fill gaps, ensuring comprehensive care. This approach ensures that you receive the best of both worlds medically, but here's an equally important reason: By registering, you can reduce the risk of penalties later in life.

5.1.2 Veterans and Medicare Late Enrollment Penalties

Yes, veterans who register for Medicare after their eligibility window will typically have to pay **late enrollment penalties** unless they qualify for specific exemptions. Here's how the rules apply (U.S. Centers for Medicare and Medicaid Services, n.d.):

Part A (Hospital Insurance):

- **Premium-free Part A:** Most people, including veterans, qualify for premium-free Part A if they or their spouse paid Medicare taxes for at least 10 years (40 quarters). There is no penalty for late enrollment in premium-free Part A.
- **Part A with a Premium:** If a veteran does not qualify for premium-free Part A and delays enrollment, then they will pay a late enrollment penalty. The penalty is 10% of the Part A premium for twice the years they delayed enrollment.

Part B (Medical Insurance):

Veterans who delay enrolling in Part B without creditable coverage (such as employer-sponsored insurance) will incur a 10% penalty for each 12 months they were eligible for but not enrolled.

This penalty is applied to the Part B premium and continues as long as the patient is enrolled in Part B.

Part D (Prescription Drug Coverage):

Veterans who do not have creditable prescription drug coverage (e.g., VA drug benefits) and delay enrolling in Medicare Part D will pay a penalty. The penalty is 1% of the national base beneficiary premium for each month they went without coverage, and is permanently added to their Part D premium.

5.1.3 Exceptions for Veterans

Veterans can avoid late enrollment penalties in the following ways:

- **They Have Creditable Coverage**:
    a. VA healthcare is considered creditable coverage for Medicare Part D (prescription drugs), meaning veterans who rely on VA drug benefits are not penalized for delaying Part D enrollment.
    b. However, VA healthcare is not considered creditable coverage for Medicare Part B. Veterans who delay Part B enrollment without other qualifying insurance (e.g., employer-sponsored health coverage) may face penalties.
- **Special Enrollment Period (SEP)**:
    a. Veterans with qualifying employer-sponsored health insurance can delay enrolling in Medicare without penalty, like their civilian counterparts, and enroll later during an SEP.
    b. This does not apply if they are solely relying on VA healthcare, as VA healthcare is not deemed

equivalent to employer-sponsored health insurance.

5.1.4 Why Veterans Should Consider Enrolling on Time

Even if a veteran uses VA healthcare services there are some important points to consider when making this decision.

- Medicare expands access to non-VA providers, especially in emergencies or when VA facilities are unavailable.
- Delaying Part B enrollment without qualifying coverage can result in lifelong penalties and higher costs.
- Veterans who decide to enroll in Medicare later in life often regret the penalties and limited enrollment options.
- Veterans are generally subject to Medicare late enrollment penalties unless they have other qualifying creditable coverage. To avoid penalties, it's recommended that veterans carefully assess their health coverage needs and consider enrolling in Medicare Parts A and B when first eligible, even if they currently rely on VA healthcare.

5.1.5 Real Example: Vince

Vince is a veteran who uses VA hospitals for primary care visits and medications. He wanted a Medicare plan that allowed him to see a highly recommended orthopedist close to his home. He did not need civilian prescription drug coverage because he liked the VA's convenient prescription mail delivery, which worked well for him. He enrolled in Parts A and B when he first became eligible due to permanent disability. After researching plans the specialist accepted, he enrolled in a Medicare Advantage (MA) plan that did NOT include prescription drugs.

If you are a Veteran getting all your meds from the VA and decide to work with an agent, you'll want to state early in the conversation that you do not need drug coverage.

Summarizing for Veterans. As you explore these options, remember that combining plans isn't just about the coverage you have today; it's also about planning for future needs, and ensuring that your healthcare remains adaptable and responsive. Whether you're transitioning from an employer plan, leveraging VA benefits, or combining both, the key lies in understanding how each piece fits together. By doing so, you can create a healthcare strategy that's not only comprehensive, but also uniquely suited to your lifestyle and health goals.

5.2 DUAL ELIGIBILITY AND CHRONIC CONDITIONS

Medicare and Medicaid are two distinct programs, yet they are often confused with each other. Again, Medicaid is a joint federal and state program that provides health coverage to eligible low-income individuals and families. It is the largest source of health insurance for people with limited income in the United States. Unlike Medicare, which is primarily for seniors and certain disabled individuals, Medicaid is designed to assist low-income families, children, pregnant women, elderly individuals, and people with disabilities.

5.2.1 Special Needs Plans: Dual Eligibility

Being dual-eligible for Medicare and Medicaid opens a unique set of benefits that can be incredibly supportive for those who qualify. Dual eligibility applies to individuals who meet the criteria for both Medicare and Medicaid, typically based on age, disability, and income level. This status provides access to a broader range of services and financial aid, often covering costs that Medicare alone does not. For many, this means reduced hospital bills, lower prescription costs, and additional coverage for services like long-term care. The combination of benefits can significantly alleviate the financial burden of healthcare, allowing you to focus on maintaining your health without the stress of mounting medical expenses.

Seniors who receive Medicaid financial assistance can collaborate with an advisor or agent who understands dual eligibility and its different rules and coverage limits, which can be complicated. Medicare and Medicaid have regulations; thank goodness thousands of experts work at CMS. State and county governments manage this partnership—also referred to as a Medicare Savings Plan (MSP), depending on who you are talking with.

These Medicaid-based plans help people with limited incomes and resources pay for Medicare premiums, deductibles, coinsurance, and copayments. State Medicaid programs fund them with different tiers and use unique acronyms, such as QMB (Qualified Medicare Beneficiary),

SLMB (Specified Low-Income Medicare Beneficiary), and QI (Qualified Individuals).

Each state administers Medicare Savings Plans through its Medicaid program. Call your state Medicaid office to inquire about eligibility requirements, and to obtain application forms or guidance on the application process.

You can find contact information for your state Medicaid office by

- Visiting the Medicaid.gov website.
- Calling 1-800-MEDICARE (1-800-633-4227)
- If applicable, getting help from SHIP (State Health Insurance Assistance Program). SHIP counselors provide free, personalized assistance to help seniors navigate MSPs and other Medicare-related questions.

Here is how to find your local SHIP office: Call 1-877-839-2675 or visit the website https://www.shiphelp.org/.

Medicare Savings Plans can provide substantial financial relief for seniors with limited income and resources. By contacting their state Medicaid office, consulting SHIP counselors, and gathering the necessary documentation, seniors can successfully find and enroll in an MSP to reduce Medicare-related expenses.

5.2.2 Real Example: James

James is an older gentleman in one of the larger West Virginian cities. He juggles Medicare and Medicaid eligibility. He is enrolled in a Medicare Advantage DE-SNP plan, which stands for Dual Eligible-Special Needs Plan. This plan has allowed him to continue his rehabilitation therapy without financial strain. This coordination of benefits provides James with peace of mind, knowing his healthcare insurance needs are met.

5.2.3 Special Needs Plans for Chronic Conditions

Having the right coverage is beneficial and necessary for individuals managing chronic conditions. Chronic illnesses like diabetes or heart disease require specialized care and consistent management to maintain quality of life. This often includes regular visits to specialists, ongoing medication, and sometimes access to durable medical equipment like glucose monitors or mobility aids. Medicare offers coverage for many of these needs, but navigating the specifics can be challenging. Understanding which services require prior authorization, how to access home health services, and what equipment is covered can alleviate much of the stress of managing a chronic condition. By staying informed, you ensure that your healthcare remains continuous and effective.

5.2.4 Real Example: Martha

Martha is a senior managing diabetes, who is also dual-eligible due to her chronic condition. She has been injecting expensive insulin for years. We found Martha a Medicare Advantage C-SNP, which refers to a Chronic Condition-Special Needs Plan. This allows her to receive regular check-ups and diabetes management supplies without incurring additional costs.

As we conclude this chapter, I encourage you to reflect on how dual eligibility and chronic condition special needs plans could enhance your healthcare experience. Understanding these aspects of Medicare allows you to tailor your coverage to meet your specific needs, ensuring you have the support necessary to maintain your health. Whether dual-eligible or managing a chronic condition, the goal is to navigate these complexities confidently, knowing that the right resources and support are available.

MAKE A DIFFERENCE WITH YOUR REVIEW

YOUR WORDS CAN HELP SOMEONE FIND PEACE OF MIND

"The best way to find yourself is to lose yourself in the service of others."

— MAHATMA GANDHI

People who give without expecting anything in return often feel the most fulfilled. Together, we can help others feel confident and calm about Medicare!

My mission with *Medicare Simplified* is to make Medicare easy to understand, straightforward, and stress-free. However, I need your help to reach more people who need this guidance.

Most people pick books based on reviews. That's why I'm asking you to leave a review and help someone else discover this book.

It won't cost a thing and takes just a moment, but it could improve someone's Medicare experience. Your review could help a new Medicare enrollee feel prepared instead of overwhelmed. Thank you for being part of this mission!

SCAN THE QR CODE BELOW AND SHARE YOUR THOUGHTS TO MAKE A DIFFERENCE:

SCAN ME

6

CHOOSING THE RIGHT PLAN

It is nice when people remember our names and appreciate that we are regular customers, whether it is your mechanic, hairdresser, or pharmacist. This kind of personal connection and consistency is what many of us seek from our healthcare providers. Ensuring access to preferred doctors and hospitals is usually crucial for most Medicare enrollees. The choice of providers in your Medicare plan can significantly impact your experience, affecting everything from the quality of care to the costs you incur.

Provider networks are a fundamental aspect of Medicare plans. These networks determine which doctors and hospitals you can visit under your plan. In-network providers have agreements with your Medicare plan to offer services at reduced rates, which can help keep your costs down. On the other hand, seeing an out-of-network provider might result in higher out-of-pocket expenses. This distinction is like dining at a restaurant where the menu prices are clearly marked versus ordering from a place with hidden fees. If you choose an out-of-network provider, you might face unexpected charges, which could strain your budget. Understanding this can guide you in selecting a plan that aligns with your healthcare preferences and financial situation.

Verifying whether your desired doctors are part of a plan's network is crucial in choosing the right Medicare plan. Fortunately, there are resources to assist you in this process. Online provider directories, often available on Medicare plan websites, allow you to search for specific doctors and hospitals to see if they are in-network. These directories function like a phone book, offering a straightforward way to check provider participation. Additionally, contacting the provider's office directly is a good idea. A simple phone call can confirm whether they accept your prospective Medicare plan. This dual approach ensures you have accurate information, helping you avoid surprises when you need care.

Continuity of care is another essential consideration. Maintaining relationships with your existing healthcare providers offers numerous benefits. While most doctors are so busy nowadays they don't remember anything about us off the top of their heads, they have our medical records. This knowledge facilitates more personalized and effective care, like a trusted mechanic who knows your car inside and out. Consistent specialist care is equally important, especially if you manage chronic conditions requiring regular monitoring and treatment. Changing specialists can disrupt your care and lead to complications, underscoring the importance of verifying their participation in your Medicare plan's network.

6.1 REAL EXAMPLE: JOAN

Joan has been enjoying her Medicare Advantage HMO plan for years. She rarely saw specialists, so getting referrals never bothered her. In September, she received a letter from her insurance company stating that her plan would no longer be available in her service area. In fact, the company was only offering Medicare Advantage PPO plans starting in 2025. Joan was worried because she appreciated the HMO's affordability and never felt constrained by the network. Her biggest concern was about staying with her doctor. She called me, and we were able to enroll her in a PPO plan that her provider's office was scheduled to accept in 2025.

As you consider your Medicare plan options, take a moment to list your current healthcare providers. Note their names, specialties, and any specific needs you have, such as ongoing treatments or medications. Any competent licensed agent will ask you for all those names; we can look them up in the official enrollment system to see if those providers will take the plans you are considering. Most good agents will even call your doctor's office. If there is any doubt, I call your provider's front desk or billing department to ask if they will accept your specific plan.

6.2 LOCATION MATTERS GREATLY

I cannot emphasize enough that where you live can significantly influence the Medicare plans available to you. The options in a bustling city will differ from those in a quiet rural town. Thanks to the dense concentration of healthcare facilities and providers, you often find a wider variety of

Medicare Advantage plans in urban areas. These plans can offer comprehensive networks because they can access a larger number of hospitals and specialists. However, the landscape changes in rural regions, where fewer providers and facilities may limit the availability of specific plans. This can mean fewer choices and potentially higher costs if you need to travel for specialized care. Understanding these geographic differences is crucial as you consider your healthcare coverage, ensuring that your plan meets not only your medical needs, but also fits the realities of your location.

State-specific regulations and policies further complicate the Medicare landscape. Each state can have its rules regarding Medigap plans and how Medicaid integrates with Medicare. For instance, some states offer Medigap policies that are not available elsewhere, which can provide significant benefits depending on your needs. How Medicaid works with Medicare can also vary, affecting the coverage options available to dual-eligible individuals. These variations mean that understanding your state's specific policies is essential for making informed decisions about your healthcare coverage. Being aware of these differences can help you navigate the complexities of Medicare, ensuring that you choose a plan that aligns with your unique needs and circumstances.

6.2.1 Real Example: John

I assisted a retiree named John, who moved from the Georgia Hill Country in the northern part of the state to DeKalb County, which is considered part of the Atlanta metropolitan area. In the countryside, his options were limited, and specialist visits required long drives, leading to frustration and delays in care. Upon moving to the city, John found a Medicare Advantage plan with a broad network of providers, offering more convenient access to necessary healthcare services. This shift improved his access to care and enhanced his quality of life by reducing travel time to medical appointments.

6.3 COMPARING ADVANTAGE PLANS

When evaluating Medicare plans, focusing on specific features that will impact your healthcare journey is essential. Consider coverage comprehensiveness and limitations—what services are included, and for what might you need to pay extra? Each plan has nuances, and understanding these can prevent surprises later. Premiums are another critical factor. While a lower premium might seem attractive initially, balancing this against potential out-of-pocket costs is crucial. Deductibles and maximum out-of-pocket expenses should also be on your radar. These elements can significantly affect your healthcare budget, making it vital to weigh them carefully. By methodically comparing these aspects, you can make a choice that aligns with your health needs and financial situation.

Another critical aspect of choosing a Medicare plan is understanding the star ratings. These ratings provide a snapshot of plan quality, ranging from one to five stars. A higher star rating indicates better service and customer satisfaction. Medicare's star rating system considers member experience, customer service, and plan performance. Higher-rated plans usually offer a better overall experience, which can be a good indicator of reliability. However, remember that even a plan with a high star rating might not best fit your unique needs. Considering all plan elements—not just its rating- is essential when deciding. Still, the star rating can serve as a helpful guide, significantly helping to narrow down your options.

6.3.1 Check with Your Specialist

Navigating the intricacies of Medicare can sometimes feel like solving a complex puzzle, especially when it comes to ensuring that your healthcare specialists are compatible with your chosen plan. Specialists are crucial in managing specific health conditions, so having the right ones in your network is vital. If your chosen Medicare plan does not include your preferred specialists, then you might pay higher out-of-pocket costs when you visit them. This can strain your finances, mainly if you rely on frequent specialist care. Imagine finding the perfect pair of shoes, only to discover they pinch after a few steps; it is much the same with choosing a plan without confirming specialist compatibility.

This is why checking whether your specialists accept your Medicare plan is necessary for your peace of mind and pocketbook. Then, all you have to know is how much your copay is to see that specialist. To confirm the copay, the first step is to contact the specialist's office directly. A quick phone call can provide the most up-to-date information on whether they accept your Medicare plan. The staff are usually familiar with the ins and outs of their network affiliations, so they can confirm participation swiftly.

Additionally, for readers with internet access, using insurance company websites can be helpful, but never go solely by what you read online. Always double check with your doctor's office. These directories list all the doctors and specialists included in a network plan, giving you a comprehensive view of your options. By utilizing these resources, you can verify specialist participation before making any commitments, ensuring a seamless integration with your healthcare needs.

Referrals are another layer to consider when dealing with specialist care under Medicare. The process can vary depending on whether you have Original Medicare or a Medicare Advantage plan. With Medicare Advantage HMO plans, referrals are usually required to see a specialist. This means that you will need a referral from your primary care physician to access specialist services, much like a ticket to enter a special event. This requirement can affect how you navigate your healthcare, potentially adding extra steps to your care process. In contrast, Medicare Advantage PPO plans and Original Medicare usually allow you to see specialists without needing referrals. Understanding these differences can help you choose a plan that aligns with your preferences and expectations for accessing specialist care.

6.3.1.1 Real Example: Jane

Consider my client Jane, who has been managing a chronic heart condition for several years. Her cardiologist has been integral to her healthcare, providing consistent and specialized care crucial to her well-being. Although Jane's condition is serious, she did not qualify for a Special Needs Plan for

Chronic Conditions. When Jane selected a new Medicare plan, ensuring that her cardiologist was in-network was a top priority. She contacted her cardiologist's office to confirm participation before calling me. She had taken notes from her conversation with her doctor's staff, so she had a concise list of plans that she wanted me to look up for her. That is a fitting example of what I mean by "research." A couple of phone calls to her provider's office was all she needed to do to feel prepared to speak with an agent!

6.3.2 Summary of Medicare Advantage Plans

When selecting a Medicare plan, your lifestyle and health goals may be a part of your decision-making process, but it should not be a primary focus. Medical insurance is a serious business designed to save your life if needed, cure you of disease and ailments, and provide preventive care and screenings.

It is great to have extra benefits that support an active lifestyle. For example, seeking a Medicare Advantage plan that includes the basic Silver Sneakers gym membership is a great idea for folks who like to go to the gym. However, if you never step foot in a gym, that is a benefit you do not have to worry about finding. Now, you may end up in a plan, for other reasons, which happens to include Silver Sneakers. There is not anything you can do to remove it, nor will you be compensated for not using it.

In short, when choosing a Medicare plan, it is crucial to prioritize medical coverage, drug coverage, and care options over extras like gym memberships or grocery cards, as these "nice-to-have" benefits will not matter if the plan does not cover your essential healthcare needs and medications.

As we've covered, Medicare Advantage (Part C) plans are private health plans approved by Medicare that provide Part A (hospital) and Part B (medical) coverage, often including Part D (prescription drugs) and extra benefits. Here's a "key features" summary for the different types of Medicare Advantage plans:

6.3.2.1 HMOs - Health Maintenance Organization

- Requires members to use a network of doctors and hospitals.
- Typically requires referrals to see specialists.
- Lower premiums and out-of-pocket costs compared to other Part C plans.
- Includes Part D prescription drug coverage unless it is a MA-only plan.

Best For: Those who prefer lower costs and coordinated care but are okay with provider network restrictions.

6.3.2.2 PPO - Preferred Provider Organization

- Offers more flexibility to see doctors inside or outside the network.
- No referrals are needed to see specialists.
- Out-of-network providers cost more but are still covered.
- Includes Part D prescription drug coverage unless it is a MA-only plan.

Best For: Those who want more provider flexibility and are willing to pay higher costs for out-of-network care.

6.3.2.3 HMO-POS - HMO Point-of-Service

- Works like an HMO but allows some out-of-network care at a higher cost.
- Typically, still requires referrals for specialists.
- Includes Part D prescription drug coverage unless it is a MA-only plan.

Best For: Those who like the affordability of an HMO but want limited out-of-network options

6.3.2.4 PFFS - Private Fee-for-Service

- Allows members to see any Medicare-approved provider that accepts the plan's payment terms.
- No network restrictions (unless the plan has a network).
- Some PFFS plans include Part D prescription drug coverage, while others do not.

Best For: Those who want more provider flexibility but need to confirm each provider's acceptance of the plan before receiving care.

6.3.2.5 SNP - Special Needs Plan

- Designed for people with specific health conditions, low income (Medicaid dual eligibility), or living in institutions.

- Tailored benefits, provider networks, and drug coverage for specific needs.
- Three types:
    - **Chronic Condition SNP (C-SNP)** – For chronic conditions like diabetes, heart disease, etc.
    - **Dual-Eligible SNP (D-SNP)** – For those eligible for both Medicare and Medicaid.
    - **Institutional SNP (I-SNP)** – For those living in long-term care facilities.

Best For: Those with specific medical, financial, or living situations needing tailored benefits.

6.3.2.6 MSA - Medical Savings Account

- Combines a high-deductible health plan (HDHP) with a medical savings account.
- Medicare deposits money into the MSA, which beneficiaries use for qualified medical expenses.
- Does NOT include Part D; members must enroll separately in a standalone Part D plan.

Best For: Those comfortable managing a savings account for medical expenses and paying a high deductible.

As you can see, each plan has different rules, provider access, and cost structures, so choosing the right one depends on your medical needs, budget, and provider preferences.

6.4 COMPARING MEDIGAP PLANS AND THEIR BENEFITS

I've mentioned Medigap policies numerous times throughout this book, and here is a summary chart of the different supplement plans. It's important that we don't confuse Medicare Advantage referred to as Part C and Medigap Supplement Plan C. Likewise there's a Supplement Plan D not to be confused with a standalone Part D drug plan.

Benefit	Plan A	Plan B	Plan C*	Plan D	Plan F*	Plan G	Plan K	Plan L	Plan M	Plan N
Part A Coinsurance and Hospital Costs	✓	✓	✓	✓	✓	✓	✓	✓	✓	✓
Part B Coinsurance or Copayment	✓	✓	✓	✓	✓	✓	50%	75%	✓	✓
First 3 Pints of Blood	✓	✓	✓	✓	✓	✓	50%	75%	✓	✓
Part A Hospice Care Coinsurance or Copayment	✓	✓	✓	✓	✓	✓	50%	75%	✓	✓
Skilled Nursing Facility Coinsurance			✓	✓	✓	✓	50%	75%	✓	✓
Part A Deductible		✓	✓	✓	✓	✓	50%	75%	50%	✓
Part B Deductible			✓		✓					
Part B Excess Charges					✓	✓				
Foreign Travel Emergency (Up to Plan Limits)			✓	✓	✓	✓			✓	✓
Out-of-Pocket Limit	N/A	N/A	N/A	N/A	N/A	N/A	$7,220 †	$3,610 †	N/A	N/A

6.4.1 Additional Medigap Notes

- **Plan C** is only available to individuals who were eligible for Medicare before January 1, 2020.
- **Plan K and Plan L**: These plans include annual out-of-pocket limits, which are indexed annually. Once you reach the out-of-pocket limit and meet the Part B deductible, the plan pays 100% of covered services for the remainder of the year.
    - **Plan K Out-of-pocket Limit**: $7,220 (2025).
    - **Plan L Out-of-pocket Limit**: $3,610 (2025).
- **Plan N**: Covers 100% of the Part B coinsurance except for copayments of up to $20 for office visits, and up to $50 for emergency room visits that do not result in an inpatient admission.

It's important to note that Medigap policies generally do not cover long-term care (e.g., care in a nursing home), vision or dental care, hearing aids, eyeglasses nor private-duty nursing.

6.4.2 Summary of Current Medigap (Supplement) Plans

For new Medicare enrollees (those who became eligible for Medicare on or after January 1, 2020), the following Medicare Supplement (Medigap) plans are available:

Plan A – Medigap Plan A is the most basic Medicare Supplement plan, offering core benefits but no additional coverage beyond what is required by federal law. It is available in all states but may have limited availability depending on the insurer. It pays Part A and Coinsurance or

Copayments but does not cover Part A and B deductibles nor Part B excess charges. Common in states like Massachusetts, Minnesota, and Wisconsin, which have their own Medigap standardization rules.

Plan B – Medigap Plan B provides the same basic benefits as Plan A, but with one important addition: coverage for the Medicare Part A deductible. It is a moderate-coverage Medigap plan that helps reduce out-of-pocket hospital costs.

Plan D – Medigap Plan D provides comprehensive coverage by filling many of the gaps left by Original Medicare (Parts A & B). It covers a variety of out-of-pocket costs but does not cover Part B excess charges. Covers 100% of Part A coinsurance for hospital stays and provides an extra 365 days of hospital coverage after Medicare benefits are used up. Pays the entire Part A deductible, which you would otherwise owe before Medicare starts covering hospital stays.

Plan G – Medigap Plan G is one of the most comprehensive Medicare Supplement plans available, covering nearly all of the out-of-pocket costs left by Original Medicare (Parts A & B) except for the Medicare Part B deductible. Covers 100% of Part A coinsurance for hospital stays and provides an extra 365 days of hospital coverage after Medicare benefits are used up. Pays the entire Part A deductible ($1,676 in 2025), which you would otherwise owe before Medicare starts covering hospital stays. It pays the 20% coinsurance that Medicare Part B does not cover for doctor visits, outpatient care, and preventive services. It covers 100% of the daily coinsurance costs for skilled nursing facility stays beyond day 20 up to day 100, which Medicare only partially covers. Plan

G is preferred by people who want minimal out-of-pocket costs beyond the Part B deductible while visiting doctors who charge excess fees, since Plan G covers Part B excess charges.

High-Deductible Plan G is similar to standard Plan G but comes with a higher deductible of $2,870 in 2025 in exchange for lower monthly premiums.

Plan K – Medicare Supplement Plan K is a cost-sharing Medigap plan that helps cover some out-of-pocket expenses while keeping premiums lower than more comprehensive plans. It covers 100% of Medicare Part A coinsurance and hospital costs, but only 50% of other key benefits, including Part B coinsurance, hospice care, skilled nursing facility coinsurance, and the Part A deductible. Unlike many other Medigap plans, Plan K has an annual out-of-pocket limit of $7,220 in 2025, which provides financial protection by capping expenses.

Plan L – Medicare Supplement Plan L is a cost-sharing Medigap plan that covers a higher percentage of costs than Plan K while still offering lower monthly premiums than more comprehensive plans. It pays 100% of Medicare Part A coinsurance and hospital costs, plus 75% of key expenses like Part B coinsurance, hospice care, skilled nursing facility coinsurance, and Part A deductible. Plan L also includes an annual out-of-pocket limit $3,610 (2025), meaning once you reach this limit, the plan covers 100% of covered costs for the rest of the year. However, it does not cover Part B excess charges. Plan L is a good option for those who want moderate cost-sharing with financial protection from high medical expenses.

Plan M – Similar to Plan D but only covers 50% of the Part A deductible and does not cover Part B excess charges. This plan is ideal for individuals who want a balance between lower premiums and solid coverage but are comfortable sharing part of their hospital deductible costs. It's important to note that not all insurance companies offer every Medigap plan, so availability may differ depending on your location. To determine if Plan M is offered in your area, you can use the Medicare Plan Finder or contact insurance providers directly.

Plan N – Lower premiums but includes copays for doctor visits ($20) and emergency room visits ($50) and does not cover Part B excess charges.

As of 2025, **Medicare Supplement Plan F is not available to new enrollees** who became eligible for Medicare on or after January 1, 2020, in any state. This restriction applies nationwide, including in states like Massachusetts, Minnesota, and Wisconsin, which have their own standardized Medigap plans. Therefore, new Medicare beneficiaries in 2025 cannot enroll in Plan F, regardless of their state of residence.

Plan G is often recommended as an alternative to Plan F because it covers nearly everything except the Part B deductible and provides full coverage for Part B excess charges.

Plan N is also popular because it has lower premiums, but it requires copays and does not cover excess charges.

7

KNOWLEDGE IS EMPOWERING

7.1 SPEAKING MEDICARE TERMINOLOGY

The purpose of this section is to explain the importance of knowing a few key terms when working with an agent, advocate or government specialist. It can make a huge difference in how empowered and knowledgeable you feel. We've covered a lot of ground quickly, so I encourage you to refer to the Glossary section frequently to revisit the most common terms used. You don't have to memorize any of this. Instead, you can use this book to circle items or to make notes. Writing down a few key Glossary terms before you call your insurance company or agent can literally save you hours.

7.1.1 Real Example: Susan

Susan called me last summer and started the conversation like this: "Hi Anne, I'm calling today because I just moved to a different part of the state to live closer to family, so I know I have to enroll in a new Medicare Advantage plan for my new location, right? I qualified for chronic special needs for the past couple of years at my old address, so I'm hoping my new plan will be the same type. My sister highly recommended her PCP and endocrinologist, so I want to select them if you can confirm they are accepting new patients." *Wow!* Susan already knew that she qualified for a Special Enrollment Period (SEP) due to her move, and for a C-SNP due to her lifelong Type 1 diabetes. She also knew the term PCP which means Primary Care Physician, and that not all doctors are accepting new Medicare patients.

7.1.2 Real Example: George

George calls and starts with, "Hi Anne, my doctor says I need Medicare." That's it; that's all he knew to say. He wasn't sure if he was already enrolled in Parts A and B and didn't have any idea what his doctor's office was requesting of him, so we started from the very beginning with his age and whether he ever received the red, white, and blue card like the one on the cover of this book. After a ten-minute search, the card was found in a kitchen drawer. Once he was able to give me his Medicare identification number and permission to look up his eligibility we were able to make progress.

Please know I'm not telling this story because it has anything to do with me. I love teaching folks about Medicare. It was a nightmare for George. No one likes feeling stupid about any aspect of their own life, yet this is exactly how millions of Americans feel every day.

Back to George, the mystery was finally solved, and it all worked out. It turned out that he was enrolled in Medicare Parts A and B, and a Part D drug plan, with the help of his wife when she was still alive, but that was it. For the past couple of years, his doctor's office has been urging him to get a Supplement plan to help cover out-of-pocket costs. The doctor ordered a colonoscopy and an upper endoscopy. This is when they scope down your throat while you are under anesthetic for the colonoscopy. George needed a Supplement plan to help cover out of pocket costs associated with this procedure. We found a Plan G that worked well within his budget. He said he felt completely relaxed about unexpected medical costs that may come up in the future.

7.2 PRIOR AUTHORIZATION

George's scenario provides a great illustration of why prior authorization is our best friend. None of us can predict every medical cost, except for the preventive services required by law, which should always have a $0 copay. However, other procedures will not be so straightforward. The medical providers always run a prior authorization in the system so they can tell you a nearly exact estimate of what you will be required to pay.

Original Medicare Part B generally covers colonoscopies as a preventive service, such as colon cancer screening. It will pay 100%, meaning no deductible or coinsurance applies. However, if the doctor finds and removes a polyp or performs a biopsy during the procedure, then it is reclassified as a diagnostic service, and 20% coinsurance and the Part B deductible may apply. If the endoscopy is done while you are an inpatient (e.g., during hospitalization), then it is covered under Medicare Part A. In George's case, he would have to pay Part A deductible (currently $1,600 per benefit period for 2025), and no coinsurance applies if he is hospitalized for fewer than 60 days.

Medicare Advantage (Part C) plans, offered by private insurers, are required by law to cover endoscopy procedures as much as Medicare Parts A and B would for the Original Medicare folks, but the cost-sharing rules may differ slightly. These plans often require a copayment (fixed amount) for the procedure and prior authorization before you can have the endoscopy. You may also face different network restrictions, meaning that you could pay higher costs if you go out of network. If you have a Medicare Advantage plan, check with your plan for specific costs, as they can vary.

Simply put, there are a lot of variables that will determine what George's out-of-pocket costs will be, such as:

- **Type of Procedure:**
    - Preventive (e.g., screening) procedures may be fully covered.
    - Diagnostic or treatment-based procedures will likely require coinsurance.

- **Facility Type:**
    - Costs may differ if the procedure is done at a hospital outpatient department, ambulatory surgery center, or doctor's office.
- **Additional Costs:**
    - If anesthesia or biopsy is needed, you may incur extra costs.
    - Pathology testing from biopsies is billed separately and subject to Medicare coverage rules.

7.2.1 Scenario 1 (Screening Endoscopy)

- Mary, age 65, undergoes a Medicare-covered screening colonoscopy.
- Medicare covers the procedure 100% as a preventive service.
- Total cost to Mary: $0.

7.2.2 Scenario 2 (Diagnostic Endoscopy)

- John, age 70, has an endoscopy to diagnose abdominal pain.
- The total cost is $1,000, and Medicare approves $800.
- John has already met his Part B deductible, so Medicare pays 80% ($640), and John pays 20% ($160).
- However, there is a remaining $200 because the provider charged more than the Medicare-approved amount ($1,000 - $800 = $200). Who pays this depends on whether the provider accepts Medicare assignment:

- If the provider accepts Medicare assignment, they must accept the $800 as full payment, meaning John only owes $160 (his 20% coinsurance).
- If the provider does not accept Medicare assignment, they can bill John for an additional amount, known as excess charges. Medicare limits these charges to 15% over the approved amount ($800 × 15% = $120). So, in this case, John would pay an additional $120, making his total out-of-pocket cost $280 ($160 coinsurance + $120 excess charge).
- Unless John has a Medigap (Medicare Supplement) policy that covers excess charges, he would be responsible for paying any excess charges himself.

7.2.3 Scenario 3 (Polyp Removal)

- Jack goes in for a screening colonoscopy, but a polyp is removed during the procedure.
- Medicare reclassifies it as a diagnostic procedure. Jack pays the Part B deductible and 20% coinsurance for the procedure.

7.2.4 George's Scenario (EGD and Colonoscopy)

Prior authorization indicated the following costs for George:

EGD Procedure Medicare-approved Amount: $1,000

Colonoscopy Medicare-approved Amount: $1,200

Total Coinsurance (20% of $2200): $440

Plus any Part B Deductible: $226 (if not yet met)

Estimated Out-of-pocket Cost: $666

In summary, the exact out of pocket costs for procedures while on Medicare depends on:

- the reason for the procedure (preventive vs. diagnostic).
- where the procedure is performed (outpatient, inpatient, or ambulatory center).
- whether you've met your deductible and your plan's cost-sharing terms.

7.3 DEDUCTIBLE

A medical deductible is the amount of money you must pay out-of-pocket for healthcare services or prescription drugs before Medicare begins to cover costs.

Here are real examples and explanations of how a medical deductible works in Medicare, with a focus on Medicare Part A, Part B, and Medicare Advantage:

7.3.1 Medicare Part A (Hospital Insurance)

Deductible for 2025: $1,676 per benefit period.

- **How It Works:** Part A deductible applies to each benefit period, not annually. A benefit period begins when you're admitted to a hospital or skilled nursing facility and ends 60 days after you leave.
- **Example:** John is admitted to the hospital for surgery in February. He pays a$1,676 deductible for this stay. Later, in September, John is hospitalized again. Because more than 60 days have passed since

his first hospital stay, this begins a new benefit period, and he must pay the $1,676 deductible again. John has a Part G Medigap plan that will pay for his Part A deductible and coinsurance, so he's not concerned.

- **Why It's Confusing:** Many people assume the deductible applies annually, like most insurance plans, but Medicare Part A resets with each benefit period.

7.3.2 Medicare Part B (Medical Insurance)

Deductible for 2025: $257 annually.

- **How It Works:** The Part B deductible is an annual deductible that applies to most outpatient services, like doctor visits, lab tests, and durable medical equipment. After meeting the deductible, you pay 20% coinsurance for covered services.
- **Example 1:** Sarah visits her doctor in January and has a $100 lab test and a $200 X-ray. The total bill is $300, but Sarah must pay the first $257 because that's her Part B deductible. After paying the deductible, Medicare will cover 80% of any additional costs, and Sarah will pay 20% coinsurance.
- **Example 2:** In June, Sarah visits a specialist, and the bill is $500. Since she already met her deductible in January, Medicare covers 80% of the cost ($400), and Sarah pays 20% ($100).
- **Why It's Misunderstood:** People often confuse the deductible with coinsurance, expecting Medicare to cover services right away. Additionally, some

preventive services (like flu shots) are covered at 100% without applying the deductible, which can create further confusion.

7.3.3 Medicare Advantage (Part C)

Medicare Advantage plans (offered by private insurers) often have their own deductibles for medical services and prescription drugs. These vary widely by plan.

- **Example:** Maria is enrolled in a Medicare Advantage plan with a $500 annual medical deductible and a $150 drug deductible.
    - In February, Maria sees her primary care doctor and a specialist, incurring $400 in medical bills. She pays the full amount out-of-pocket because she hasn't met her $500 medical deductible yet.
    - In April, she needs an MRI costing $800. Maria pays the remaining $100 to meet her deductible, and the plan pays 80% of the remaining cost ($560). Maria pays the other 20% ($140).
    - Maria also fills a prescription costing $200 in May. She must pay $150 to meet her drug deductible, and her plan covers the remainder ($50).
- **Why It's Misunderstood:** Medicare Advantage deductibles often combine with other cost-sharing elements (like copays), making it hard for enrollees to understand when and how their deductible applies.

7.3.4 Medicare Part D (Prescription Drug Coverage)

Deductible for 2025: Example $505 annually (varies by plan).

- **How It Works:** The Part D deductible applies to prescription drug costs. You must pay the full cost of your prescriptions until you meet the deductible, after which you pay only copays or coinsurance.
- **Example:** Robert's Part D plan has a $505 deductible. He fills a $100 prescription in January and another $150 prescription in February, paying the full cost each time. By March, after filling a $300 prescription, Robert has met his $505 deductible. For the rest of the year, he only pays small copays (e.g., $10 per generic drug).
- **Why It's Misunderstood:** Many people think the deductible applies to all prescriptions equally, but some plans exclude lower-cost generic drugs, meaning those may not count toward the deductible.

7.3.5 Key Points to Remember

- Part A deductibles reset per benefit period, while Part B and Part D deductibles reset annually.
- Medicare Advantage plans have their own rules and deductibles that vary by plan.
- Preventive services often bypass the deductible, leading to confusion about when costs apply.
- Tracking deductibles can be challenging due to different billing systems and timelines for claims processing.

7.4 MOOP (MAXIMUM OUT-OF-POCKET)

The Maximum Out-of-pocket (MOOP) is the highest amount you must pay in a year for covered healthcare services under a Medicare Advantage plan. Once you reach this limit, your plan pays 100% of the costs for covered services for the rest of the year. MOOP applies to your out-of-pocket expenses for covered services, including deductibles, copayments, and coinsurance.

MOOP does not include monthly premiums, prescription drug costs (covered under Part D), or services not covered by your plan.

7.4.1 In-network vs. Out-of-network

For plans with network providers, there may be separate MOOP limits for

- in-network costs (lower MOOP).
- out-of-network costs (higher MOOP or no limit).

Example:

- You're enrolled in a Medicare Advantage plan with a $5,000 MOOP for in-network services.
- Throughout the year, you pay
  - $1,000 in deductibles.
  - $1,500 in copayments for doctor visits.
  - $2,500 in coinsurance for a hospital stay.

- Total Out-of-pocket: $5,000
- Once you reach the $5,000 MOOP, your plan covers all remaining in-network costs for the rest of the year.

MOOP is an important number to know when enrolling in a Medicare Advantage plan because it protects you from unlimited expenses for covered services. Different Medicare Advantage plans have different MOOP limits, but Medicare requires no plan to exceed $8,300 for in-network services (2025 limit). MOOP acts as a financial safety net, ensuring you won't pay beyond a certain amount for covered health-care services in a year.

8

AGENTS, ADVOCATES, AND RESOURCES

Imagine stepping into a busy library—shelves lined with books, offering a wealth of knowledge. Each volume holds answers to your Medicare questions. It's so overwhelming that you feel like turning around immediately and leaving. Until your personal librarian, someone who knows exactly where all the information is, offers to assist you. This is the role of a licensed Medicare agent—to guide you through the intricate maze of Medicare options, making sure you arrive at the correct destination for your healthcare needs. In the future, I will use the term licensed agent interchangeably with advocate. Sometimes, different insurance companies and agencies refer to their licensed agents as advocates. Medicare agents and advocates provide invaluable services, offering one-on-one consultations to help you understand the various plans. They can assist with enrollment, ensuring you make the most informed choices possible. Whether you're grappling with the complexities of Medicare Advantage plans or trying to decipher the nuances of Medigap, agents or advocates stand ready to offer clarity and direction.

Working with a Medicare agent or advocate is not just about gaining information; it's about personalized support. These experts tailor their advice to your unique situation, considering your health needs, financial circumstances, and personal preferences. The reassurance that comes from having expert support can transform the Medicare experience from daunting to reassuring.

Importantly, I recommend working with licensed agents over anyone else in your community. Here's why: licensed agents have access to all the different systems full of information, and because we comply with the strict laws regarding Medicare, you're more likely to avoid predatory practices.

8.1 LAWS GOVERNING MEDICARE ENROLLMENTS

I'm including this material in the book to put minds at ease about how strict the laws are for Medicare agents. We all know the terrible stories; I hear them all the time. There are real slime balls out there screwing up people's lives, and it's all illegal. I know good agents who have reported some of these bad actors to CMS, but they can handle only so much crime stoppage. We must help them, and I will tell you how you can do so. I also maintain that knowing the information in this chapter will help you work with agents and advocates more efficiently.

8.1.1 Calls Recorded

CMS (Centers for Medicare & Medicaid Services) now requires that all phone calls are recorded in their entirety between Medicare beneficiaries and agents or brokers, as long as they are related to Medicare Advantage (MA) and Prescription Drug Plan (PDP) marketing, sales, and enrollment. This requirement took effect on October 1, 2022, as part of the updated CMS Medicare Communications and Marketing Guidelines (MCMG). Most importantly, for understanding our next section, this includes calls where Scope of Appointment (SOA) forms are obtained verbally.

Agents or organizations must also securely store the recordings for 10 years and make them accessible if CMS requests them during audits or investigations. At the beginning of the call, agents must inform the beneficiary that the call is being recorded. A typical disclosure might be: "This call is being recorded for quality and compliance purposes."

Agencies and third-party marketing organizations (TPMOs) must also comply with this requirement when interacting with beneficiaries. An example of an exception would be In-person meetings and appointments, which are not subject to this requirement. The recording requirement only applies to telephonic interactions.

This rule was introduced to improve transparency and protect beneficiaries from misleading or fraudulent marketing practices. It also provides an audit trail for compliance and dispute resolution, ensuring agents adhere to CMS regulations during interactions.

8.1.2 Scope of Appointment

Medicare agents and brokers are subject to specific requirements and regulations established by CMS to ensure compliance and protect consumers. One key aspect is the Scope of Appointment (SOA) requirement, which governs how Medicare agents interact with beneficiaries. Here's a breakdown of the requirements and laws:

Agents must obtain a Scope of Appointment agreement before every conversation. There are multiple ways to achieve this, the most notable of which is the call recordings explained above.

The SOA is a documented agreement that outlines the topics an agent may discuss with a Medicare beneficiary during a meeting. It ensures transparency and protects beneficiaries from unsolicited or high-pressure sales tactics. It's to help protect you from predatory bait-and-switch practices. Imagine calling to enroll in a standalone Part D plan, but instead, you were enrolled in an Advantage plan and an optional supplemental dental plan after you hung up. Optional Supplemental Benefits (OSBs) are not to be confused with Original Medicare Supplement policies. Think of an OSB as an opportunity to give yourself a Booster dental plan by paying extra monthly.

There are several ways SOAs are obtained nowadays. Each method must comply with CMS guidelines to ensure transparency, accountability, and proper documentation. Below are the most common ways Medicare agents can obtain SOAs:

- Paper forms can be completed and signed before the appointment.
- An SOA can be completed and signed electronically via a secure system. This is becoming more prevalent because agents can use CMS-compliant platforms or software that allow beneficiaries to sign the SOA form electronically.
- Verbal consent can be obtained when the client verbally agrees with the SOA during a recorded phone call.
- An SOA form can be submitted online through a secure portal. Agents provide a link to the SOA form hosted on a CMS-compliant platform. Beneficiaries fill out the form and electronically sign it.
- Lastly, there's fax or email submission, which is when clients can send a completed SOA form via fax or email. Agents email or mail the SOA form to the beneficiary for them to fill out, sign out, and return using fax or email.

8.1.3 Regulations for Medicare Agents

By now, you probably understand how Medicare agents must comply with strict CMS rules to maintain their licensure and ensure ethical practices. Agents must be licensed in their respective states and complete annual training and certification for the Medicare products they help people enroll in. They cannot engage in unsolicited calls or visits without prior consumer consent. No door-to-door marketing. No cross-selling of non-healthcare-related products during Medicare appointments. All marketing and sales materials must be CMS-approved before use. When enrolling their clients, agents must provide accurate and unbiased information and assist beneficiaries in making informed choices. They must not pressure beneficiaries into enrolling in a plan. Agents must disclose their relationship with the insurance company and whether they are paid a commission for sales. The penalties for non-compliance can lead to suspension or revocation of licensure and financial penalties, termination of contracts with insurance carriers, and even criminal charges in cases of fraud or severe violations. While CMS sets the overarching rules, some states may have additional requirements for agents, such as state-specific continuing education or consumer protection laws.

8.1.4 Meetings and Educational Events

The rules and regulations around Medicare marketing and educational events are also strict. For starters, the event must be registered with CMS. The registration process typically involves the insurance carriers (Medicare Advantage or Prescription Drug Plan sponsors) the agent represents, who report these events to CMS. It must be registered as a marketing or educational event. The plan sponsor is responsible for submitting event details to CMS through the Health Plan Management System (HPMS). Most plan sponsors require agents to provide event details at least 10-14 days in advance to allow timely submission to CMS.

The rules for each type of event are extensive, so I'll give you a short version. For educational events, information must be neutral and cannot include sales or plan-specific details. For marketing events, agents may discuss specific plans, distribute enrollment materials, and collect applications, but must adhere to marketing rules.

8.1.5 Real Example: Dorothy

Dorothy is a retiree transitioning from employer insurance to Medicare, felt overwhelmed as she approached her 65th birthday. Her neighbor had given her my name and number, so Dorothy phoned me. I then emailed over an SOA agreement for Dorothy to complete. Dorothy wanted to discuss ALL her options, such as Original Medicare, Part D policies, Medigap policies, and Medicare Advantage Plans. She listed all that on the form, signed, scanned it with her printer, and emailed it back to me for our Zoom appointment. Dorothy lived in a rural area with only one community hospital and her doctor's practice. She had already asked them which carriers they accepted, making this even easier. She selected a standalone Part D drug plan and Plan G for her supplement. We reviewed the entire Summary of Benefits and a few other details, so she knew what to expect, and she was done.

8.1.6 Real Example: Joe

Joe faced complex billing issues that frustrated him. He phoned his Advantage plan insurance company and asked for an advocate's assistance. That person explained everything so Joe could understand his billing statements, identify errors, and work with his providers to correct them.

Both examples highlight how calling and talking with Medicare experts can make Medicare an easy-to-understand journey.

8.2 USING ONLINE RESOURCES

Imagine having a toolbox filled with the precise instruments you need to navigate Medicare; each tool is designed to simplify your experience and enhance your understanding. For those of you with internet access, you can explore a large array of online resources.

8.2.1 Medicare's Website

Medicare's official website (**https://www.medicare.gov/**) is a cornerstone in this digital landscape, offering a comprehensive Plan Finder tool that helps you explore and compare various Medicare plans. I highly recommend everyone start their Medicare journey with this tool. This tool allows you to input your current prescriptions, preferred doctors, and other personal preferences to see which plans offer the best coverage for your needs and in your zip code. This can be a quick source of empowerment through knowledge.

8.2.2 List of Medicare Insurance Carriers

Here is a list of Medicare insurance carriers and their URLs. If I missed anyone, please email me at Anne@Medinsure.one so I can include it in the next edition of this book:

- **Aetna Medicare: https://www.aetnamedicare.com/**

- **Anthem: https://www.anthem.com/medicare/**
- **Blue Cross Blue Shield: https://www.bcbs.com/medicare**
- **CareFirst Med Plus: https://www.carefirst.com/**
- **Centene Corporation: https://www.centene.com/**
- **Cigna: https://www.cigna.com/medicare/**
- **Cigna Health Spring: https://www.cigna.com/medicare/**
- **Colonial Penn: https://www.colonialpenn.com/**
- **Devoted Health: https://www.devoted.com/**
- **Highmark Health: https://www.highmark.com/**
- **Humana: https://www.humana.com/medicare**
- **Kaiser Permanente: https://medicare.kaiserpermanente.org/**
- **Manhattan Life: https://www.manhattanlife.com/**
- **Medico Insurance Company: https://www.gomedico.com/**
- **Mutual of Omaha: https://www.mutualofomaha.com/medicare-supplement**
- **Philadelphia American Life Insurance Company: https://www.neweralife.com/**
- **State Farm: https://www.statefarm.com/insurance/medicare-supplement**
- **UnitedHealthcare: https://www.uhcmedicare.com/**
- **USAA: https://www.usaa.com/inet/wc/insurance_medicare_solutions**
- **WellCare: https://www.wellcare.com/**
- **Zing Health: https://www.myzinghealth.com/**

8.3 IN-PERSON AND PHONE RESOURCES

Medicare also has an official helpline at 1-800-MEDICARE.

State Health Insurance Assistance Programs, or SHIPs, offer another support system. These programs provide free, impartial counseling on Medicare options. They are available nationwide and offer a wealth of information about state-specific laws, especially regarding Medicaid and Medicare dual-eligible enrollees.

Community workshops on Medicare topics are another valuable resource. These workshops, hosted by knowledgeable professionals, delve into various aspects of Medicare, from enrollment processes to understanding different plan options. These sessions offer a structured environment where you can ask questions, but if you feel like you are in an aggressive sales presentation that is pushing one company or type of plan, keep your guard up because that's not allowed. On the bright side, it may be an opportunity to find a local agent who offers in-person appointments.

8.4 MUST READ - INSURANCE PLAN LETTERS

The best advice I can give regarding letters from insurance companies or Medicare entities is to carefully read all correspondence from CMS, your insurance company, and healthcare providers at least twice before worrying. Here's why I say this: Medicare-related letters can be immediately unsettling for some seniors, often causing anxiety before they've even read the first few sentences. These communications are typically formal, impersonal, and written in a standardized format, making them feel cold and difficult to interpret.

They are mass-generated form letters, not personalized messages, which can sometimes add to the confusion.

Most of the time, when a client is near tears on the phone, it's because of something that came in the mail. Multiple times every day during the Annual Enrollment Period (October 15–December 7), someone calls to say, "Why have I been dropped by my Medicare Advantage plan?" I know exactly which letter they received. They have not been dropped; they received a ***Plan Discontinuation Letter*** and simply need to enroll in a new plan that will take over for their current plan starting January 1st. Medicare plans are occasionally discontinued just like old battle ships are decommissioned. Again, this has nothing to do with you personally. Just like the battleship example, usually there's no need for concern because new battleships have already rolled off the dock.

8.4.1 Medicare Annual Change Notice

The Medicare Annual Notice of Change (ANOC) is a letter sent every fall (by September 30th) to Medicare beneficiaries who are enrolled in a Medicare Advantage (Part C) or Medicare Part D (prescription drug) plan. This letter comes from your insurance company and outlines any changes to your plan's costs, coverage, and rules for the upcoming year. It is important to review this notice carefully to ensure your plan still meets your needs.

What's Included in the ANOC Letter?

Premium Changes – Whether your monthly payment is increasing or decreasing.

Deductible & Copay Adjustments – Any updates to how much you'll pay out-of-pocket for doctor visits, hospital stays, or prescriptions.

Coverage Changes – Modifications to what's covered, such as changes to drug formularies, provider networks, or specific benefits.

Rule Changes – New requirements like prior authorizations for certain medications or procedures.

Your Next Steps – Information on open enrollment (October 15 – December 7), when you can switch plans if needed.

Why does the ANOC Letter Matter? Even small changes in your plan's coverage or costs can impact your healthcare expenses, so it's crucial to read this notice carefully and compare your options before Medicare's Annual Enrollment Period (AEP).

9

AVOIDING SCAMS AND FRAUDULENT SCHEMES

It's important to understand that these schemes are more common than many realize, and they often target the most vulnerable seniors. That said, I've heard stories from people of all demographics, ages, genders, and educational backgrounds. If you've been tricked into switching plans, please know you are in the company of millions. The reason is that fraudsters are just so good at their craft. They have no qualms about misleading and lying to confuse seniors so they can make a fast buck. By familiarizing yourself with scammers' tactics, you can protect yourself and maintain control over your Medicare benefits.

9.1 PHONE SCAMS

One of the most prevalent scams involves phone calls from individuals posing as Medicare representatives. These callers often use high-pressure tactics, creating a sense of urgency to trick you into revealing personal information. They might have a problem with your account, or you must update your information to avoid losing benefits. This is a ploy to gather your Medicare number and other personal details for fraudulent activities. It's crucial to remember that Medicare will never call you uninvited to ask for personal information. If you receive such a call, hang up immediately. Do NOT engage in the conversation. If you put a toe in that snake pit, they will verbally wrap around your neck and choke you into submission. People engage when they know to hang up because the fraudsters use a tiny bit of accurate information that sounds so "relevant" to your situation. They call and say, "We noticed your plan is increasing your drug deductible this year; we can help you find a much better plan with a premium that will never go up." Once you hear words like "premium will never go up," that's a red flag. Real agents don't make false promises.

Every year, from early October until December 7, we are bombarded with nonstop commercials telling us to call to evaluate our coverage. Some people think they ***have to*** call every year because of those ads. I know they are hard to ignore, but they are designed to lure you into making unnecessary phone calls. They are misleading and cause significant confusion and distress for millions of seniors yearly. If you are happy with your Medicare coverage, then there's no reason to call yearly. Your plan will auto-renew. Again, if you do not receive a Change Notice letter from your carrier stating changes you cannot tolerate, it's a great idea to stick with your current plan. If you do not receive a discontinuation letter, then your plan will auto-renew on January 1 every year. If you are happy with your coverage, do NOT make phone calls. Some scammer agencies will have you twisted into knots and second guessing your own name.

Usually, they are only paid if they switch you to a different plan, so please understand their motives. You cannot believe everything you hear on TV, especially regarding Medicare.

9.2 MEDICAL SUPPLIES SCAMS

Another common scam is the offer of free medical supplies or services. Scammers will promise free COVID-19 tests or medical devices, claiming they just need your Medicare number to process the order. Once they have your information, they can bill Medicare for services or supplies you never received, leaving you with unexpected charges and complications. These offers seem appealing, especially when they promise something for nothing, but they are often too good to be true. Always verify any offer with Medicare directly before providing any personal information.

9.3 SPOOFING SCAMS

Scammers often spoof caller IDs to make their calls appear legitimate. Spoofing involves disguising a phone number to make it look like it's coming from a trusted source, like Medicare or a healthcare provider. This can make it difficult to discern what's real and what's not. The scammers rely on creating panic and urgency, pushing you to make quick decisions without taking the time to verify their claims. They might insist that you act immediately to avoid penalties or loss of coverage, playing on your fears to manipulate you into compliance.

9.3.1 Real Example: Irene

Consider the story of Irene, a senior who received a call from someone claiming to represent Medicare. The caller told her that her account was at risk due to suspicious activity, and that she needed to confirm her Medicare number to secure her benefits. Concerned and wanting to resolve the issue, Margaret provided her details, only to later discover unauthorized charges on her account. This type of scam can have serious financial and emotional consequences, leaving victims feeling violated and anxious.

To protect yourself, always verify the legitimacy of any communication you receive regarding Medicare. Check for an official Medicare letterhead and contact information on any correspondence. If you receive an unsolicited offer or request for information, contact Medicare directly to confirm its authenticity. This simple step can prevent scammers from taking advantage of you, and also help you maintain control over your personal information.

9.4 PROTECTING YOUR PERSONAL INFORMATION

Each piece of data—your Social Security number, Medicare ID, date of birth, and other personal details—is referred to as PII. PII (Personally Identifiable Information) refers to any information that can be used to identify an individual, either on its own or when combined with other data. It includes details that can be directly linked to a person, or that could indirectly identify them. When exposed, personal information can be used to commit fraud, leaving you vulnerable to financial and emotional distress. Think of it this way: Your

Social Security number and Medicare ID are keys to your identity and keeping them secure is your best defense against identity theft.

Technology is pivotal in protecting your information, offering tools that enhance security measures. Implementing two-factor authentication on your online accounts is a wise decision and is usually required nowadays. This means that even if someone gets hold of your password, they would still need a second form of verification to access your account, like a code sent to your phone. This added layer of security can prevent unauthorized access and give you peace of mind. Additionally, installing reputable antivirus software on your devices can help protect against malware and phishing attacks. These programs can detect and neutralize threats before they cause harm. In a world where digital threats are ever-present, leveraging technology to your advantage is an effective way to safeguard your personal information.

9.5 FRAUD PREVENTION: RECOGNIZING RED FLAGS

Imagine answering your phone to a friendly voice—one that sounds trustworthy, claiming to be from Medicare. This person starts asking for your personal details, maybe your Medicare number or Social Security number. It's easy to feel caught off guard, especially when they insist it's for updating your records or resolving an issue with your account. Such calls can rattle anyone, but they should immediately raise a red flag. Unsolicited calls requesting personal information are a hallmark of fraudulent schemes. It's crucial to remember that Medicare will never call you to ask for your personal information out of the blue. Offers that seem too good to be true, like free services or products, often come with strings attached. These can be deceptive tactics to gather your information under false pretenses.

Skepticism can be your ally in these situations. When faced with unfamiliar or unexpected communications, approach them with a healthy dose of caution. Cross-reference any information you receive with official Medicare resources. Verify the credentials of individuals offering services, especially if they seem eager to secure your personal information. The internet can be a valuable tool here; use it to check if the company or individual is reputable. This due diligence can save you from potential scams, and help you maintain control over your personal details. Always remember, it's better to be safe and take the time to verify than to rush and regret it later.

9.5.1 Real Example: John

I remember John. He was happily going about his retirement life with zero concerns regarding Medicare. He loved his Medicare Advantage PPO plan. His providers accepted the plan, and he had zero complaints. He only had a house phone with no caller ID, so he picked up most calls if he could. He picked up the phone one afternoon in November during AEP, and thought he was talking with a real Medicare agent or Medicare itself; he wasn't. The caller was offering a new healthcare plan that promised extensive benefits at a low cost. ***John provided his Medicare identification number as part of "hearing the guy out" and to be polite, even though he wasn't interested in making a change.*** He ended the call and didn't think anything of it until he received a letter welcoming him to a completely different insurance company and plan. This happens all the time. Unless you are genuinely shopping for Medicare solutions there's no reason to give anyone your Medicare Identification number.

9.5.2 Real Example: Helen

This is one of the worse cases I've dealt with, and I will never forget Helen because the perpetrator was someone in the community. Helen was a 90-year-old who lived in a pseudo assisted/independent living community that was connected to a senior community center in some way. Helen is a widow, more vulnerable to confusing conversations because her husband always took care of the insurance matters. Also, like so many seniors, she's lonely and always eager to be included socially.

One of her fellow residents had invited their niece into the lobby to assist all the residents in switching Medicare plans to an unknown company; there were promises of food cards and other allowances. The organizing resident put a lot of pressure on her fellow residents to switch over to the plan her niece was representing by indicating that "everyone was doing it because it was kind of required now by the community they all lived in." Helen went along because she didn't want to upset the popular woman who was the orchestrator of this pop-up enrollment event. She didn't want to have a confrontation with anyone about anything, let alone Medicare. Every single aspect of this situation was wrong and out of compliance. Helen was confused and frustrated when she realized she had been switched to a different plan.

She couldn't remember if she declined the offer at the time or if she signed anything. She desperately wanted to remain in the coverage she'd had for years because it always worked well for her. She was able to call 1-800-MEDICARE and tell them what happened. Of course, they arranged for her to be returned to the plan of her choice. Also, if this happens to you regarding your Medicare Advantage plan you can call in early January and be switched to the Advantage plan of your choice for a February 1st start date.

9.6 REPORTING FRAUD: HOW TO TAKE ACTION

Recognizing the signs of Medicare fraud is only the first step. Taking action swiftly is also crucial in minimizing its impact and helping stop the perpetrators. If you suspect fraud, the first thing to do is contact Medicare's fraud hotline at 1-800-MEDICARE (1-800-633-4227). This line is dedicated to addressing concerns and can guide you on the next steps. When you call, be prepared to provide detailed information. The clearer and more specific you are, the easier it will be for Medicare to investigate the issue. Alongside this, filing a report with the Federal Trade Commission (FTC) at ReportFraud.ftc.gov is another essential step. The FTC collects these reports to detect patterns of wrongdoing, which aids law enforcement agencies in their investigations.

9.7 VIGILANCE: KEEPING YOUR MEDICARE SAFE

Think of vigilance as your personal shield—a way to protect your Medicare benefits from those who would misuse them. By regularly reviewing your Medicare statements, you can catch unauthorized charges before they spiral out of control. This isn't just about numbers on a page; it's also about ensuring that your healthcare is accurately reflected, and that your benefits are used only for your needs. Take time each month to go over your statements. Look for anything that seems off or unfamiliar. Sometimes, a single charge can be a clue to a larger issue.

Staying informed about new scam tactics and trends is equally important. Scammers are always adapting, finding new ways to deceive. By keeping up with the latest information, you arm yourself with the knowledge needed to spot these threats before they affect you.

As we wrap up this chapter, remember that staying alert and informed is your best defense against scams. Your vigilance not only protects you but also contributes to a safer environment for everyone. This proactive approach ensures that your Medicare benefits remain secure, allowing you to focus on your health without the added stress of fraud.

In the next chapter, we will explore important notices regarding bills and claims.

10

TRACKING BILLS AND CLAIMS

10.1 MEDICARE SUMMARY NOTICE (MSN)

For Original Medicare folks, another important piece of mail you will usually receive every 3 months is a Medicare Summary Notice (MSN) which is a document that summarizes your recent healthcare services and their associated costs. It's sent by CMS and lists services received, what Medicare paid, and what you owe. At first glance, the MSN might appear daunting, filled with unfamiliar terms and numbers.

The MSN is divided into several sections, each detailing specific aspects of your medical services and charges. It typically includes information about the services you received, the amounts Medicare approved and paid, and what you may still owe. This breakdown is crucial for verifying that the services you were billed for match those you received. For example, the MSN will list each service, the date it was provided, and the provider's name. It also shows the amount charged by the provider, the amount Medicare approved, and what Medicare paid. Understanding these sections helps you identify any discrepancies or errors, allowing you to address them promptly.

Reading and verifying your MSN requires careful eyes and some patience. Start by cross-checking the services listed against your personal medical records. Ensure that the dates and types of services correspond to those you received. This step helps to catch duplicate charges or services that were billed but not provided. Next, verify the accuracy of the provider information and the amounts billed. Errors in these areas can lead to incorrect charges or denied claims. Contact the provider's billing office for clarification if you notice any inconsistencies. Keeping a detailed record of your medical appointments and treatments can simplify this process, making it easier to spot potential errors.

Common errors on MSNs can include duplicate charges for the same service or incorrect coding, leading to denied claims. For instance, a physician might inadvertently submit a duplicate claim for a service, resulting in a denial. Similarly, coding errors, such as using an invalid procedure code or mismatched service dates, can cause confusion and rejection. These mistakes are common, but they can be resolved promptly. Identifying these errors early can prevent future billing issues and ensure that your healthcare costs are accurately reflected.

Consider the following scenario: You receive an MSN showing a charge for a hospital stay longer than you remember. By cross-referencing your personal records, you realize that the charge includes an extra day you didn't spend in the hospital. After contacting the billing department, you confirm the error and have it corrected, saving yourself from paying for services you didn't use. Or perhaps you notice a charge for a procedure that was never performed. Upon investigation, you discover it was a clerical error, which is quickly resolved once brought to the provider's attention.

These examples highlight the importance of understanding the claims process and being proactive in managing your healthcare expenses. Whether you're tracking claim status online, communicating with providers, or appealing a denial, each step you take brings you closer to ensuring that your healthcare needs are met without unnecessary financial stress. It's about being informed, staying organized, and knowing that you have the tools to navigate the Medicare system confidently.

10.2 EXPLANATION OF BENEFITS

Medicare Advantage (Part C) enrollees do not receive a Medicare Summary Notice (MSN) like those with Original Medicare (Parts A & B). Instead, Medicare Advantage members receive a similar document called the Explanation of Benefits (EOB) from their private insurance company that administers their plan. It's usually sent out monthly and like the MSN it lists services received, what the plan paid, and what you owe. An EOB is **not a bill**, but it helps you understand how your plan processed your claims. If you didn't use any healthcare services, you may not receive an EOB that month. Medicare Advantage plans have different rules, costs, and networks so the EOB layout may vary by insurance provider however most follow a standard format with the following sections.

1. Summary of Services & Costs

- **Statement Period** – The dates covered by this EOB.
- **Total Charges** – The full cost of the services before insurance adjustments.
- **Amount Paid by Your Plan** – The portion covered by your Medicare Advantage or Part D plan.
- **Your Responsibility** – The amount you owe, including copays, coinsurance, or deductibles.

2. Details of Medical Services or Prescriptions

A breakdown of each claim processed during the statement period, usually in a **table format**, including:

- **Date of Service** – When you received care or filled a prescription.
- **Provider or Pharmacy Name** – The doctor, hospital, or pharmacy that provided the service.
- **Service or Drug Name** – Description of the medical service or medication.
- **Total Cost** – The full charge before insurance applies coverage.
- **Plan Discount** – Any discount negotiated by the insurance company.
- **Amount Covered** – How much your plan paid toward the cost.
- **Your Share** – What you owe, such as a **copay, coinsurance, or deductible** amount.

3. Deductible & Out-of-Pocket Tracking

- **Your Year-to-Date Costs** – A summary of how much you've spent toward your **deductible and out-of-pocket maximum** for the year.
- **Remaining Out-of-Pocket Limit** – How much more you need to pay before your plan covers 100% of covered costs (if applicable).

4. Important Notes & Appeals Information

- **Claim Denials or Adjustments** – If a service wasn't covered or paid differently than expected, an explanation will be provided.
- **How to File an Appeal** – Instructions on what to do if you believe a claim was **incorrectly denied or underpaid.**
- **Customer Service Contact Info** – Your insurance company's phone number for any questions.

You should always review your EOB to ensure you were billed correctly and that no unauthorized services were charged. This statement helps track your out-of-pocket costs and deductible status. Lastly, the EOB identifies claim denials so you can file an appeal if necessary.

10.3 STRATEGIES FOR MANAGING OUT-OF-POCKET EXPENSES

Managing healthcare costs is vital to maintaining financial health, especially when you're on Medicare. A thoughtful approach to budgeting for out-of-pocket expenses can make all the difference. Begin by estimating your annual health-care costs based on your past spending. Review previous years' medical bills and records to identify recurring expenses or treatments. Knowing what you typically spend each year gives you a foundation to predict future costs more accurately. It's also wise to set aside specific savings for medical expenses. This dedicated fund acts as a buffer, providing peace of mind that you can handle unexpected medical bills without financial strain. You might consider allocating a portion of your monthly budget to this fund, like setting aside savings for other predictable expenses.

Importantly, if you find yourself with hospital or provider bills that will cause you to struggle financially, then call the hospital or medical facility and ask for a zero-interest payment plan or payment plan of any kind. I'm not saying these are always available, *but you should ask.* Explain to them the financial difficulty you are experiencing and see if they will work with you.

One of the simplest yet most effective ways to utilize these benefits is by taking advantage of preventive services and screenings. These services are often covered at no additional cost and can play a crucial role in detecting health issues early when they are most treatable. Regular check-ups, flu shots, and screenings for conditions like diabetes are all part of this preventive package to help you stay on top of your health, allowing you to address potential concerns before they become serious problems.

If you're enrolled in a Medicare Advantage plan, then you might have access to additional wellness programs. These programs often include fitness classes, nutrition counseling, and even gym memberships. Embracing these offerings can enhance your overall well-being, providing not just physical health benefits, but also a sense of community and support. Participating in such programs can be both motivating and rewarding, helping you maintain a healthy lifestyle while enjoying activities you love. It's a unique aspect of Medicare Advantage plans that goes beyond traditional healthcare, focusing on holistic health.

Coordinating your care is another key aspect of maximizing your Medicare benefits. It's important to schedule routine check-ups and follow-up appointments. This proactive approach helps prevent complications and ensures that any health issues are managed effectively. Additionally, fostering communication between your healthcare providers can make a significant difference. When your doctors and specialists share information, they can collaborate on your treatment plan, ensuring that you receive comprehensive care. This coordination minimizes the risk of overlapping treatments or medications, keeping your healthcare streamlined and effective.

CONCLUSION

Thank you for walking with me through the intricate world of Medicare. As we've explored together, understanding Medicare doesn't have to be overwhelming. Throughout this book, we've unraveled its complexities, from the basics of enrollment and eligibility to the nuances of choosing the right plan. We've tackled common misconceptions, explored the importance of preventive services, and examined strategies for managing costs effectively. Each chapter has aimed to equip you with knowledge and confidence as you navigate Medicare.

Remember the key takeaways as you reflect on the journey we've shared. First, Medicare is not a one-size-fits-all solution. When selecting a plan, it's essential to evaluate your healthcare needs, your preference for PCPs and Specialist, and your financial situation. Whether you're considering Original Medicare, Medicare Advantage, or Medigap plans, your choice should align with your personal circumstances.

Second, understanding the timing of enrollment and the potential penalty for delays is crucial. Timely decisions can save you from unnecessary expenses.

Now that you're armed with this knowledge, I encourage you to take proactive steps. Review your current Medicare plan and assess if it still meets your needs. If you're approaching the enrollment period, consider using the tools and exercises we've discussed to compare your options thoroughly. Reach out to a licensed health insurance agent or advocate if you need personalized guidance. Their expertise can provide clarity and ensure you make informed decisions.

I also invite you to share this book with anyone and everyone. I've tried to provide a more conversational and relaxed approach to inform everyone that you don't have to become a Medicare expert to feel good about your decisions. There are so many protections in place at the federal and state level.

Last but not least, I also want to express my gratitude to you. I am deeply thankful for your trust in me to guide you through this complex topic. As a licensed health insurance agent, I am passionate about helping individuals like you navigate Medicare confidently. Your questions, feedback, and experiences are invaluable to me. They help me serve clients better and enrich our shared understanding of Medicare. Please feel free to reach out anytime at Anne@Medinsure.one Your voice matters, and I want to hear about your experiences.

I hope this book has empowered you to approach Medicare with newfound confidence and clarity. As we conclude, let me reassure you that staying engaged with Medicare is a lifelong activity. Consider subscribing to newsletters or updates that provide timely information about Medicare changes. These resources can keep you informed and prepared for any adjustments needed in your plan. Remember, knowledge is your greatest ally in navigating Medicare's evolving landscape!

MAKE A DIFFERENCE WITH YOUR REVIEW

YOUR WORDS CAN HELP SOMEONE FIND PEACE OF MIND

> *"The best way to find yourself is to lose yourself in the service of others."*
>
> — *MAHATMA GANDHI*

People who give without expecting anything in return often feel the most fulfilled. Together, we can help others feel confident and calm about Medicare!

Would you lend a hand to someone like you who is curious about Medicare but unsure where to begin?

My mission with *Medicare Simplified* is to make Medicare easy to understand, straightforward, and stress-free. However, I need your help to reach more people who need this guidance.

Most people pick books based on reviews. That's why I'm asking you to leave a review and help someone else discover this book.

It won't cost a thing and takes just a moment, but it could improve someone's Medicare experience. Your review could help a new Medicare enrollee feel prepared instead of overwhelmed.

If you found this book helpful and believe it provided 5-star advice, I'd truly appreciate your review! Your feedback supports my work and helps others make informed decisions about Medicare. Please take a moment to share your thoughts here:

SCAN ME

Your kindness can create a ripple effect, empowering others to take charge of their Medicare choices just like you did. Thank you for being part of this mission!

GLOSSARY

Annual Enrollment Period (AEP): This period occurs from October 15 to December 7 each year, and it allows Medicare beneficiaries to enroll in or make changes to Medicare Advantage and Part D plans which take effect January 1 of the following year. A person can switch to or from Original Medicare to a Medicare Advantage approach.

Children's Health Insurance Program (CHIP): A program offering health coverage to children in families with incomes too high for Medicaid but too low to afford private insurance.

Chronic Special Needs Plan (C-SNP): A type of Medicare Advantage Plan tailored for individuals with specific severe or disabling chronic conditions.

CMS (Centers for Medicare & Medicaid Services): A federal agency within the U.S. Department of Health and Human Services (HHS) responsible for administering key national healthcare programs, including Medicare, Medicaid, the Children's Health Insurance Program (CHIP), and the Health Insurance Marketplace.

Coinsurance: Your share of the costs of a covered healthcare service, calculated as a percentage (e.g., 20%) of the allowed amount for the service.

Copay (Copayment): A fixed amount you pay for a covered healthcare service after you've paid your deductible.

Dual Eligible: Individuals who qualify for both Medicare and Medicaid benefits.

Dual Eligible Special Needs Plan (D-SNP): A type of Medicare Advantage Plan for individuals eligible for both Medicare and Medicaid.

End-stage renal disease (ESRD): Permanent kidney failure requiring dialysis or a kidney transplant.

Formulary: A list of prescription drugs covered by a prescription drug plan or another insurance plan offering prescription drug benefits.

General Enrollment Period (GEP): This period occurs from January 1 to March 31 each year, and it allows individuals who didn't sign up for Medicare Part B during their Initial Enrollment Period, to enroll in Part B. This also applies to individuals who need to buy Part A.

Health Insurance Marketplace: A platform established under the Affordable Care Act (ACA) to help individuals and families find and purchase affordable health insurance coverage.

In-network (IN): Refers to healthcare providers or facilities that are part of a health plan network with which it has negotiated discounted rates.

Initial Enrollment Period (IEP): The seven-month period when you're first eligible to sign up for Medicare, starting three months before you turn 65, including your birth month, and ending three months after.

Medicaid: A joint federal and state program that helps with medical costs for individuals with limited income and resources; it also offers benefits not typically covered by Medicare, like long-term care.

Medicare Advantage (Part C): An alternative to Original Medicare offered by private companies approved by Medicare, providing all Part A and Part B services and often including Part D (prescription drug) coverage and additional benefits.

Medicare Beneficiary: An individual enrolled in the Medicare program and receives its benefits.

Medicare Prescription Payment Plan (M3P): A program that allows Medicare beneficiaries to spread out-of-pocket prescription drug costs over the year to manage expenses more effectively.

Medigap (Medicare Supplement Insurance): Private insurance policies that help pay some of the healthcare costs that Original Medicare doesn't cover, such as copayments, coinsurance, and deductibles.

Open Enrollment Period (OEP): The Medicare Advantage Open Enrollment Period (OEP) runs from January 1 to March 31 each year and allows individuals already enrolled in a Medicare Advantage (Part C) plan to make a one-time change. During this period, you can switch to a different Medicare Advantage plan or drop your Medicare Advantage plan and return to Original Medicare (Parts A & B), with the option to enroll in a standalone Part D prescription drug plan.

Optional Supplemental Benefits (OSBs): Additional benefits or services policies offered exclusively to Medicare Advantage (MA) plan members beyond what is covered by Original Medicare (Part A and Part B).

Original Medicare: The traditional Medicare program, including Part A and Part B, is offered directly through the federal government.

Original Medicare Supplement Plans: Also known as Medigap policies, these are standardized plans sold by private companies to cover gaps in Original Medicare coverage.

Out of Network (OON): Refers to healthcare providers or facilities not contracted with a health plan, often resulting in higher out-of-pocket costs for the beneficiary.

Part A (Hospital Insurance): Covers inpatient hospital stays, care in a skilled nursing facility, hospice care, and some home health care.

Part B (Medical Insurance): Covers certain doctors' services, outpatient care, medical supplies, and preventive services.

Part D (Prescription Drug Coverage): Optional Medicare coverage for prescription medications, available through private plans approved by Medicare.

Personally Identifiable Information (PII): Any information that can be used to identify an individual on its own or when combined with other data. It includes details that can be directly linked to a person or that could indirectly identify them.

Premiums: The periodic payments you make to Medicare or a health plan for coverage.

PCP (Primary Care Provider): A doctor or healthcare provider who acts as the first point of contact for your healthcare needs. They coordinate your care and can refer you to specialists if necessary.

Provider: A doctor, healthcare professional, or facility licensed to provide healthcare services.

Qualified Disabled and Working Individual (QDWI): A Medicaid program that helps pay for Medicare Part A premiums for certain disabled and working beneficiaries under 65.

Qualified Medicare Beneficiary (QMB): A Medicaid program that helps pay for Medicare Part A and B premiums, deductibles, coinsurance, and copayments for eligible individuals.

Qualifying Individual (QI): A Medicaid program that pays for Medicare Part B premiums for individuals with limited income; funding is limited and granted on a first-come, first-served basis.

Scope of Appointment: A document that outlines the topics to be discussed during a meeting with a Medicare beneficiary, ensuring that only agreed-upon products are discussed.

Social Security Retirement Benefits: Monthly payments from the Social Security Administration to eligible retirees based on their earnings history.

Special Enrollment Period (SEP): Times outside the standard enrollment periods when you can sign up for Medicare or change your plan due to specific life events, such as moving or losing other insurance coverage.

Specialist: A doctor who focuses on a specific area of medicine or a group of patients who diagnose, manage, prevent, or treat certain symptoms and conditions such as a Cardiologist, Oncologist, Endocrinologist, Gastroenterologist, Orthopedist, Orthopedic Surgeon, Ophthalmologist, etc.

Specified Low-income Medicare Beneficiary (SLMB): A Medicaid program that pays for Medicare Part B premiums for individuals with limited income and resources.

State Health Insurance Assistance Program (SHIP): A state program offering free, personalized counseling and assistance to Medicare beneficiaries and their families.

REFERENCES

Age Options. (n.d.). *How to read a Medicare summary notice (MSN).* https://www.ageoptions.org/wp-content/uploads/2022/10/SMPHowToReadMSN.pdf

American Cancer Society. (n.d.). *Key statistics for colorectal cancer.* https://www.cancer.org/cancer/types/colon-rectal-cancer/about/key-statistics.html

Anthem. (n.d.). *Medicare Part D changes 2025.* https://www.anthem.com/medicare/learn-about-medicare/medicare-part-d-changes-2025

Area Agency on Aging Palm Beach. (n.d.). *Medicare.* https://www.aaapbtc.org/medicare

Blue Cross Blue Shield of Massachusetts. (n.d.). *10 common Medicare myths dispelled.* https://medicare.bluecrossma.com/learn/medicare-basics/myths

Bunis, D. & Lankford, K. (2021, October 11). *10 common Medicare mistakes to avoid.* https://www.aarp.org/health/medicare-insurance/info-2019/common-medicare-mistakes.html

Federal Trade Commission. (n.d.). *Protect your personal information from hackers and scammers.* https://consumer.ftc.gov/articles/protect-your-personal-information-hackers-and-scammers

Federal Trade Commission. (n.d.). *ReportFraud.ftc.gov.* https://reportfraud.ftc.gov/

Finley Engineering Company. (n.d.). *175,000 U.S. households still rely on dial-up internet.* https://finleyusa.com/175000-u-s-households-still-rely-on-dial-up-internet/

Gans, E. A., van Mun, L. A. M., de Groot, J. F., van Munster, B. C., Rake, E. A., van Weert, J. C. M., Festen, S., & van den Bos, F. (2023, November). *Supporting older patients in making healthcare decisions: The effectiveness of decision aids; A systematic review and meta-analysis. Patient Education and Counseling, 116.* https://www.sciencedirect.com/science/article/pii/S0738399123003610

Houston-Galveston Area Council. (n.d.). *Medicare benefits counseling.* https://www.h-gac.com/area-agency-on-aging/medicare-benefits-counseling

Lankford, K. (2023, November 15). *8 scams that senior Medicare patrols are seeing.* https://www.aarp.org/money/scams-fraud/info-2023/most-common-medicare-scams.html

Lankford, K. (2022, June 7). *How are Medigap and Medicare Advantage different?* https://www.aarp.org/health/medicare-qa-tool/medigap-vs-advantage.html

Lansey, D. (2013, April). *Avoid the most common claims errors in Medicare billing.* American College of Physicians. https://immattersacp.org/archives/2013/04/coding.htm

Lockett, E. (2022, September 13). *Medicare and employer insurance coverage.* https://www.healthline.com/health/medicare/medicare-and-employer-coverage U.S. Centers for Medicare & Medicaid Services. (2025). *Medicare and you handbook 2025.* https://www.medicare.gov/publications/10050-medicare-and-you.pdf

McGinty, B. (2023, March 2). *Medicare mental health coverage: What changed and what remains.* The Commonwealth Fund. https://www.commonwealthfund.org/publications/explainer/2023/mar/medicare-mental-health-coverage-included-changed-gaps-remain

Medicare Interactive. (n.d.). *Medicare interactive.* https://www.medicareinteractive.org/

National Council on Aging. (2023, October 30). *How do I stop a Medicare scam?.* https://www.ncoa.org/article/5-warning-signs-of-a-medicare-scam-and-how-to-protect-yourself/

National Council on Aging. (2024, February 27). *Medicare savings program eligibility and coverage.* https://www.ncoa.org/article/medicare-savings-programs-eligibility-coverage/

National Council on Aging. (2024, January 2). *Medicare enrollment periods: A guide for older adults.* https://www.ncoa.org/article/medicare-enrollment-periods/

National Council on Aging. (2023, April 7). *Understanding changes to Medicare enrollment periods in 2023.* https://www.ncoa.org/article/understanding-changes-to-medicare-enrollment-periods-in-2023

National Council on Aging. (2023, October 23). *What are the Medicare star ratings?* https://www.ncoa.org/article/medicare-star-ratings/

National Council on Aging. (2024, August 12). *Who is the best person to talk to about Medicare?* https://www.ncoa.org/article/who-is-the-best-person-to-talk-to-about-medicare/

National Council on Aging. (2023, April 7). *Medicare enrollment periods in 2023.* https://www.ncoa.org/article/understanding-changes-to-medicare-enrollment-periods-in-2023/

National Archives. (n.d.). *Medicare and Medicaid Act (1965).* https://www.archives.gov/milestone-documents/medicare-and-medicaid-act

National Council on Aging. (2022, August 6). *How Medicare covers telehealth services.* https://www.ncoa.org/article/how-medicare-covers-telehealth-services/

U.S. Centers for Medicare & Medicaid Services. (n.d.). *Chronic condition special needs plans (C-SNPs).* https://www.cms.gov/medicare/enrollment-renewal/special-needs-plans/chronic-conditions

U.S. Centers for Medicare & Medicaid Services. (n.d.). *CMS: Home - Centers for Medicare & Medicaid Services.* https://www.cms.gov/

U.S. Centers for Medicare & Medicaid Services. (n.d.). *CMS updates Medicare Advantage value-based insurance design.* https://www.cms.gov/newsroom/press-releases/cms-updates-medicare-advantage-value-based-insurance-design-vbid-model-2019

U.S. Centers for Medicare & Medicaid Services. (n.d.). *Compare Medigap plan benefits.* https://www.medicare.gov/health-drug-plans/medigap/basics/compare-plan-benefits

U.S. Centers for Medicare & Medicaid Services. (n.d.). *Compare original Medicare & Medicare Advantage.* https://www.medicare.gov/basics/get-started-with-medicare/get-more-coverage/your-coverage-options/compare-original-medicare-medicare-advantage

U.S. Centers for Medicare & Medicaid Services. (n.d.). *Explore your Medicare coverage options.* https://www.medicare.gov/plan-compare/

U.S. Centers for Medicare & Medicaid Services. (n.d.). *5 things you need to know about signing up for Medicare.* https://www.cms.gov/training-education/find-provider-type/employers-unions/top-five-medicare-enrollment

U.S. Centers for Medicare & Medicaid Services. (n.d.). *Legislative update.* https://www.cms.gov/medicare/regulations-guidance/legislation

U.S. Centers for Medicare & Medicaid Services. (n.d.). *Medicare Advantage geographic variation - national & state.* https://data.cms.gov/summary-statistics-on-use-and-payments/medicare-geographic-comparisons/medicare-advantage-geographic-variation-national-state

U.S. Centers for Medicare & Medicaid Services. (n.d.). *Medicare health plans that lower costs.* https://www.medicare.gov/basics/costs/help/medicare-lower-costs

U.S. Centers for Medicare & Medicaid Services. (n.d.). *Medicare prescription drug eligibility and enrollment.* https://www.cms.gov/medicare/enrollment-renewal/part-d-enrollment-eligibility

U.S. Centers for Medicare & Medicaid Services. (n.d.). *Medicare's coordination of benefits.* https://www.medicare.gov/publications/11546-coordination-of-benefits.pdf

U.S. Centers for Medicare & Medicaid Services. (n.d.). *Original Medicare (Part A and B) eligibility and enrollment.* https://www.cms.gov/medicare/enrollment-renewal/original-part-a-b

U.S. Centers for Medicare & Medicaid Services. (n.d.). *Understanding your Medicare Advantage plan's provider network.* https://es.medicare.gov/publications/11941-understanding-your-medicare-advantage-plan.pdf

U.S. Centers for Medicare & Medicaid Services. (n.d.). *Your guide to Medicare preventive services.* https://www.medicare.gov/publications/10110-your-guide-to-medicare-preventive-services.pdf

U.S. Centers for Medicare & Medicaid Services. (n.d.). *World of Medicare glossary.* https://www.cms.gov/Outreach-and-Education/MLN/WBT/MLN9329634-WOM/wom/PDFs/MLN9329634_WOM_Glossary_2022_508.pdf

U.S. Department of Health and Human Services. (n.d.). *HHS primer: The Medicare appeals process.* https://www.hhs.gov/sites/default/files/omha/files/medicare-appeals-backlog.pdf

U.S. Department of Veterans Affairs. (n.d.). *Eligibility for community care outside VA.* https://www.va.gov/resources/eligibility-for-community-care-outside-va/

Vision Retirement. (2024, August 7). *How to transition from private health insurance to Medicare.* https://www.visionretirement.com/articles/transitioning-to-medicare-from-private-health-insurance

www.ingramcontent.com/pod-product-compliance
Lightning Source LLC
LaVergne TN
LVHW022047200926
848481LV00003B/820